WILL SELF

SORE SITES

●●●ellipsis

This book is dedicated to Louise Rogers,
editor of *Building Design*, without whom
these pieces would not have been written

First published 2000 by
●●● ellipsis
www.ellipsis.com

© 2000 Will Self

British Library Cataloguing in Publication
A CIP record for this book is available
from the British Library

ISBN 184166031 0
Printed in Hong Kong

●●● ellipsis is a registered trade mark of
ELLIPSIS LONDON LIMITED
2 Rufus Street, London N1 6PE

CONTENTS

NOTE

These essays and drawings first appeared in *Building Design*, a weekly newspaper for architects.

S

'Gimme the paper dart! – It's my turn to be Foster …'

WORLD OF CARPET

I rolled over in bed groaning this morning. 'Eurgh,' was the tenor of said groan, 'I've got to get up and do my first *Building Design* column of the year.' My wife, who is on the receiving end of these eructo-bulletins, took this one in good enough part. 'What's it going to be about?' she enquired. 'Norman Foster,' I cleared my throat, 'I read a long profile of him the other day in *The Guardian* ...' 'Oh did you now!' She drew herself upright on a twisted dais of duvet, at once entirely alert. You see, the meat of the matter had shifted – as far as she was concerned – from architecture to newspapers. She continued: 'When I was editing *Weekend* we ran a profile of Foster – Liz Jobey wrote it; that can have been all of eight months ago!'

You see, for my wife repetition of pieces in newspapers is one of the great sins; I mean nothing so undercuts the idea that you're reading tomorrow's fish and chip paper as simultaneously viewing an all-singing all-dancing television advertisement for it. It's farragos such as this that have driven the wife away from editing and into writing columns for *The Independent* newspaper. With Deborah doing two columns a week and myself on two as well, the house has become positively neoclassical. Not that this has led to any upsurge in her interest in architecture. She still resolutely maintains that most of the aesthetic, and even functional, problems of our built environment could be solved at one fell swoop, by painting everything white.

Cladding is her especial enemy; show Deborah a council block about to be cladded and she'll reach for an old English sheepdog and dunk it unceremoniously in a ten-litre can of Sandtex. So steeped have I become in this inverse Rolling Stones fantasy, that when I dream of sinister, corporate fascist organisations, who're despatching helicopter gunships to turn me into steak mince (this, as you can imagine, is an almost nightly occurrence), the gunships always emerge from an extensively recladded council block on the South Lambeth Road.

But I digress – this is my New Year's resolution: more digression, more animadversion, more tergiversation; anything but stick to the point. It transpires, having read this immensely long profile of Sir Norman, that he flies his own private jet in between his various ongoing architectural projects. So what? you may ask. I mean, wouldn't you expect an artistic entrepreneur who operates on a global scale to get around in this fashion? What did I expect, a powered skateboard?

No, but it just so happens that before Christmas I had my first experience of riding on the flight deck of a commercial jet, and pretty heady it was too. For a start I got to witness the realities of Heathrow traffic control, and discovered that it's as much of a problem marshalling the behemoths on the ground, as it is ensuring they don't achieve conflagration when aloft. The SAS flight to Stockholm I was aboard had to be guided through several heavy junctions, crowded with other jets, before getting anywhere near the runway.

But my main insight was that from the well-appointed

front seat of a vehicle with a top speed of 600 miles an hour, the world becomes a much smaller place. Europe looks like a bosky little village, with the winking lights of Berlin, or Paris, or Budapest, approximating to the pub, the Spar convenience store, and the church, respectively.

No wonder Sir Norman favours this means of transport. Up aloft in his private jet, powering his way from one gargantuan yoghurt pot to the next, the whole of the globe must meld with his CAD-CAM brain. How I envy him as he sets up his building blocks on the rucked carpet of the world! It must impart such a marvellous sense of control, of influence, of power even; to find oneself aloft and actually able to view simultaneously two giant domes which you've been responsible for constructing.

All I can say is that it's lucky Sir Norman is a sensitive, liberal soul, completely unlike the unkind near portrayal of him in Phillip Kerr's novel *Gridlock*. I don't imagine that being able to survey the nascent, united Europe in this fashion makes him feel the slightest surge of *Übermensch*-style arrogance. *Au contraire*, I should think it only serves to make him feel uneasy when he spots the similarities between the dome of the reconstructed Reichstag, and the dome of the Tate Gallery. I wonder if, by any chance, they may be related?

'OK, granted, your tower is bigger than mine, but you're a fully qualified, 37-year-old civil engineer ...'

THE SEER OF SHEPPERTON

I was being a bit flippant last week about Sir Norman Foster. I was imagining that his world view must be dominated by the fact that when he lifts off from City Airport in his private jet, *en route* for Berlin, he may well receive the impression – as he mounts to 35,000 feet over a strangely cloudless Western Europe – that the entire continent is a vast sandpit, within which his buildings are the only truly salient objects.

I also mentioned that Sir Norman had not altogether been pleased by the parallels between himself and the megalomaniacal architect in Phillip Kerr's dystopian novel *Gridlock*. I haven't read Kerr's book, but as I understand it the gist of the plot is that said architect designs and builds an enormous high rise, which is jam-packed full of the latest technology. Everything in this building is computerised from the Venetian blinds to the waste disposal and back again. And lo and behold, the thing begins to revolt against its master, becoming mysteriously sentient and subjecting its inhabitants to the ultimate sick building syndrome.

If Sir Norman's upset at the parallels between him and Kerr's protagonist, I daresay Kerr himself is even more upset at the parallels which have been drawn between his book and J G Ballard's 1975 masterpiece *High Rise*.

Unlike most writers who are loosely bracketed under the heading 'science fiction', Ballard has never set himself up as a futurist. Rather than writing about the dialectic of technological advancement and its impact on human social forms, Ballard has always defined himself as a chronicler of 'inner space' and attempted to imagine what the parameters of the human psyche will be like in the not-so-distant future. The irony is that the works he has produced have turned out to be far more accurate predictions of the character of evolving modern life, than those written with that intention.

Nowhere is this more evident than with *High Rise*. The opening line of the novel (one of the best ever, I think) contains all of its dark promise: 'Later, as he sat on his balcony eating the dog, Dr Robert Laing reflected on the unusual events which had taken place within this huge apartment building during the previous three months.' Laing, like so many middle-class professionals, both before and since, has taken the lure offered by the prospect of high-rise, serviced living. He has purchased an apartment in a revolutionary new building, designed and built by the reclusive genius Anthony Royal.

The building is 40-storeys high, and contains, along with a thousand apartments, a full panoply of services: restaurants, night clubs, bars, shops, etc. etc. 'Delighted by this glut of conveniences, Laing made less and less effort to leave the building.' He's not alone; the other tenants also fall under the spell of the building's self-containment, and in the process turn in upon themselves. The building's vertical socio-stratification, with the poorer tenants on the lower floors, the wealthier on the higher, becomes the catalyst for increasing disruption and unease. When the actual mechanics of the high rise begin to malfunction, the latent tensions between the tenants are translated into out-and-out warfare.

Ballard's intention in this novel was – as far as I can surmise – not to present a simpleminded critique of high-rise
urban living, but to do something far more subtle. After
all, while Anthony Royal's gleaming behemoth is
described in distinctly glowing terms, the city it stands
apart from is plangently threatening: 'By contrast with the
calm and unencumbered geometry of the concert hall and
television studios below him, the ragged skyline of the city
resembled the disturbed encephalograph of an unresolved
mental crisis.'

No, Ballard's target is far bigger: it's the whole notion of
planned urban development as an aspect of overarching
social planning. Elsewhere in his work Ballard returns to
this theme again and again, and perhaps it's no accident
that several of his protagonists have been architects. While
his vision of a war between the occupants of different
floors of an enormous high rise may not have become literally true (though I daresay there are some high-rise
dwellers who've experienced near warfare), one aspect of
High Rise has done.

In the novel Anthony Royal's gleaming new building is
located quite specifically: 'For all the proximity of the city
two miles away to the west along the river ...' Yes, you
guessed it: in 1975 Ballard foretold the construction of
Canary Wharf. Now that's what I call science fiction!

'It's Lord Rogers – for you!'

SMART BOMB IN A TEASHOP

Puttering down from the Vale of Pershore, where we've been spending the weekend, the biggest noticeable change in the *echt*-zone that is the Cotswolds is the bypass which has finally been built to reroute the A44 around the village of Broadway. This will excise a piece of cod-anachronism once and forever from the space-time continuum which is the rest of the country.

Broadway, with its honeyed manses lined up along its plump, pillowy verges, has to be the last word in Cotswold ditsiness; an hideous assemblage of tea shops, card shops, gift shops and crap shops. The whole souk of kitsch doubtless retailing small toby jugs which, when you smack yourself in the forehead with them, make you feel as if you're a piece of leather just bludgeoned by some tempered willow. Betjeman called down friendly bombs on Slough, Morrissey entertained the notion of a first strike against Blackpool: 'This is the coastal town that they forgot to drown/ Come, come nuclear war ...', but I'd be prepared to make a case for a pre-emptive one against Broadway.

In 1991, during the Serbian war on Croatia, it was widely feared that the historic city of Dubrovnik would be severely damaged by shelling – and lo and behold it was. Those bloody Serbians! Absolutely no capability for smart bombing whatsoever; thick as Acrow props. Now if it had been NATO at work, Jamie Shea, or some other user-friendly PR minion (remember in the Falklands 'conflict' the MOD mouth was dubbed 'the speaking clock' – shows you how focus groups have changed the world for the better), would be telling us how our laser-targeted bombs were wiping out this piece of jerry-built, 1970s sub-brutalism, while leaving that superb romanesque church with its incomparable vernacular frescos, miraculously intact.

If NATO were – accepting the inevitable fissioning of the Alliance itself – to launch air strikes against Middle England, I daresay, like me, their commanders might well contemplate the Broadway option. After all, Broadway epitomises the forces – tourism, merchandising, the bogusness of advertising, nostalgia – that are at the very core of our nation's command and control structures, and is thus an entirely justifiable target. Yes, I know that some people are going to complain, say I'm being sick, unfunny, vilely puerile, but I can't help it if these more deadly thumps, bangs, and airborne pollutants come just at the time that the village has finally been delivered from the bombardment of the artics – you should never have had that hysteria about wisteria in the first place.

Oh, all right, I withdraw it. There's nothing that smart about bombing Broadway. But what would be really intelligent would be to bomb the old Valley Tweed Mill in Chipping Norton, just up the road. This foursquare piece of late nineteenth-century patronisation (1872) has the dubious distinction of making it into the pages of Felipe Fernandez-Armesto's masterful summation of the era, *Millennium,* as follows: 'an outstanding example of a "cathedral of industry"'… has not been enhanced by its recent conversion to "luxury flats". The developers' concept, however, of the mill as a setting for a privileged, rural way

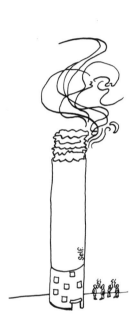

of life, was consistent with the ethos of late nineteenth-century factory building, which imitated palatial traditions in architecture. The publicity emphasises the sporting facilities and healthy amenities. The showhouse is decorated in a pastiche of the English "country house" style.'
And now get in there and make some tweed, you bastards! Except, of course, that the latter part of the above applies to potential luxury-flat occupants, rather than the sweated schmutter workers of yore. The fact remains that it's a building which is superficially attractive – you can't fail to notice it as you drive through – yet never invites a closer examination. That's because its initial conception was just as bogus as the eventual use to which it's been turned. My wife said that what Fernandez-Armesto describes as an 'elegant tapering chimneystack', reminds her insistently of a 'lovely fag'; and her aesthetic judgements are second to no one's.

Anyway, I don't have to justify the bombardment: our NATO bombs are smart enough to smell this out – and warn all the occupants to evacuate in time. Of this I am resolutely certain. Until the next briefing.

NONE OF THIS WILL BE YOURS

What a grand week it's been for me in architecture. I read a round-up in *The Independent* of the millennium projects which are now slated to be late; another piece informed me that share prices in German construction firms were rocketing (ha! ha!) in anticipation of contracts to rebuild Serbia; and lastly I discovered the enormous flea market which is cradled within the New Covent Garden Market at Nine Elms.

Sunday morning was nice and bright and I decided to take Will Jnr for a push in his chair around the 'hood. We headed across the Wandsworth Road and through Sainsbury's car park. At the back of this there's a gate which gives access to a strange hinterland where the service roads for the Nine Elms Market intersect with the mainline into Waterloo. I should've noticed something was up at this juncture, because there were a fair number of bag-porting people streaming through the gate and heading off in the direction of the market buildings, but instead I took the foot tunnel under the railway and headed for the embankment.

Standing by the show house for the absurd St George's Wharf apartments, we looked across the river to the northern, property-encrusted shore. 'Some day son,' I told Will Jnr, 'none of this will be yours. After all, any one of those houses we can see has a generous six-figure price tag, and they stretch along the river front from here to Chiswick and beyond. Whereas on our side of the river, there's nothing but the stark beauty of the post-industrial landscape, together with some modest blocks of 1980s apartments.'

It was a view that doesn't feature much in film or television: the Thames, looking west along the south bank from central London. This must be – it occurred to me as we strolled on – because it isn't on the narrow path which most television and film producers travel in life – from Islington to Soho, to Shepherd's Bush, to the Cotswolds.

As we reached the waste treatment centre, hard against the sad bulk of Battersea Power Station (which really should be zoned for luxury apartments now, anything to stop further decay), we were forced back on to the main road; and here we saw still larger streams of pedestrians, all flowing towards the fruit and vegetable market. We joined them and sauntered back under the railway line and into the odour of many many tons of moribund vegetable matter.

London's great greens entrepôt is as uninspiring a piece of architecture as it's possible to imagine. I suppose it could be argued that there's no necessity for a market to have any particular aesthetic merit – but surely only by the philistines who built this one. It comprises several long ramparts of enormous corrugated-iron shed. That's it: big boxes made out of off-colour ticky-tacky, and surrounding them a lot of tarmac.

Rounding the end of one of these massive hangars we came upon the Mecca which was gathering in all these hurrying people. It was a huge flea market. There must have been well over a thousand stalls thronging the defile between the permanent market buildings. These weren't chi-chi displays of knick-knacks or tourist gee-gaws; they were the workaday essence of exchange at the base of the economic pyramid. Old geezers in from Essex with two old power tools lain out on a table cloth; wide boys from wherever with a transit load of plastic toys; and mobile snack bars pumping out big baps full of pork roast – the kind which would be called 'barms' up north.

Granted, I've only lived in the area for a couple of years, and granted also that I have all the neighbourly chit-chat skills of Mike Tyson on angel dust, but nevertheless this degree of local ignorance still stunned me. One short walk and two revelations: a view I'd never seen represented anywhere; and an enormous souk of which I'd never heard tell. One of these had been denied me because of the way our proscenium view of the built environment is framed by the media; the other had been hidden from me for reasons of class. Yup, class. For this flea market was an exclusively working-class affair, a teeming confluence of people who don't flood out of the city at the weekend, but on the contrary pour in from the poor outer-London suburbs to sell stuff to the people in the poorer inner-London suburbs. The bourgeoisie would never dream of attending, save for a little retail slumming.

Village London? That's in Roseland.

'It's a brown-nose site – so, if you don't mind ...'

STOCK BRICKIES

My brother, who used to be notorious as the Junk Mail King of London, once told me that he had calculated that the overall volume of junk mail he was responsible for producing was equal to that of the Great Pyramid of Cheops. Naturally, the anecdote was told in a spirit of self-deprecation, and consummate irony – but is it really that funny?

All those printers, all those envelope stuffers (a righteously tedious job; I know, I've done it), all those postmen, and all for what, a shot on bin? To be involved in this useless chain would have to be the ultimate indignity of labour. But on the other hand, to suggest that labour has any intrinsic dignity may be just as ridiculous.

The erection of a great deal of scaffolding in my street this week has led me to ponder once more my own career as a labourer. There was that, and there was actually walking past – for the first time in many years – a house on which I laboured.

I had answered an advert in the paper for hod carriers; although, as a spindly-shanked, pizza-faced nineteen-year-old, I was about the same weight and shape as a hod. They laughed at me and set me to mixing the mortar, then shifting alternate loads of it, together with bricks, in a wheelbarrow. The site was about a quarter of an acre of ditches, mud and planks. The house under construction was for a super-brickie who had got his mates in to do the laying in rapid-fire shifts of about an hour each.

These guys were working so fast that if you narrowed your eyes you could watch the walls rising like something filmed in a stop-action sequence. The only thing holding up this highspeed erection was the laughably slow brickies' mate, and boy was I laughed at.

At the end of that day I was not simply in physical pain from every stretchable part of my body having been yanked apart; I was in psychic pain as well. I could see that I was quite simply unfit for this kind of work, unable to keep it up, and by implication unfit to hold up my head in society. I stuck it for a few more days and then collapsed back into adolescent sopor and torpor.

But I remained obsessed by the idea that there might be some dignity in labour; or rather, that by being able to physically labour, I might either validate or fatally undermine my utter preoccupation with carrying weighty ideas around in my head. After I left university I got a job as a driver-cum-labourer for a general builders' firm, a job I managed to hold down for about eight months (which probably makes it one of the longest jobs I've ever had).

I learnt to tell a putlock from an Acrow prop, and a London from a stock brick. I learnt the location of the vast, secret hinterland of builders' merchants that exists in every city – but most importantly I learnt how to labour.

Labouring – as I was informed in no uncertain terms by my colleagues – is all about pacing; it's all about attempting to judge the correct ratio of energy-to-time necessary to complete the given task with the least overall effort. A good labourer will manifest the evidence of this approach in the smallest of his actions as well as his largest. He will always lift a long piece of scaffolding at precisely the right fulcrum point, just as he will always drag and then tip a fifty-kilo bag of ballast. Over an hour, a day, a week, or a lifetime, the good labourer will conscientiously seek to minimise every physical expenditure, so as to avoid exhaustion.

It's not fanciful to suggest that the very act of limiting yourself in this sphere is one that also leaves you prone to limiting yourself in others. The labourer's lowly social status is as much an acknowledgement of this fact as it is an example of the harsh invidiousness of the division of labour itself.

Or to put it another way: labourers are often called upon to appreciate the architecture of the buildings that they build, but the reverse is never the case.

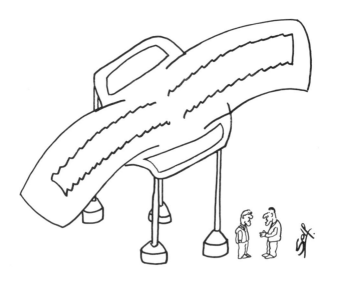

'You can tell by the wings that it's the Bodyform Building ...'

PEOPLE IN GLASS MINDS

'Can you tell me what this building is called please?' 'Called?' Her eyes were doubly myopic: imprisoned behind the security glass of her booth, and secured behind the miniature booths of her glasses. 'This building … what's its name?' 'Building?' I began to feel panicky. I had fully expected the security guard at the door of MI6 to deny that this was in fact MI6, but was she further attempting to deny that there was a building here at all as a necessary prelude to denying that this conversation ever took place? 'Yes, what's this building called?' 'This is the Foreign Commonwealth Office.' She was comfortable with this absurd, tautologous ascription, and for that matter so was I. I strolled off for a walk round this most obvious of secret premises.

Dominating the southern end of London's Vauxhall Bridge, the spec. building by Terry Farrell and Associates which now houses the British secret service is the kind of place from where Dr No might have run his operation, had he diversified his evil empire into airline catering services and office equipment supplies. The building is a ghastly pastiche of an office block: from the river side, myriad levels of blank windows ascend and retreat, to form a bathetic ziggurat. At the middle level of the façade there is a single enfilade of what look like – I kid you not – poplar trees, which are just crying out for the Startrite kids to go tripping along them. The flanks of the building are apparently dominated by giant, upended Rotadexes; and at the top of this joke monumentalism there is another, giant Rotadex. Behind this two finial towers protrude like the book ends of Pantagruel. The whole edifice isn't helped by being dressed with stone that has an unappealing, dried snot texture and colour.

Really this building's most obvious influence is the banjaxed 1940s-into-1980s set designs for Terry Gilliam's film *Brazil*; which was – ironically enough – about a man grappling with a bizarre fascist regime obsessed by secrecy and bureaucracy.

Courtesy of Lambeth Council you can walk along the river side of the 'Foreign Commonwealth Office' and admire the faux Japanese garden they've constructed. I did so this morning but found it deserted save for a dosser eating some sandwiches. Looking up at the ranks of green-tinted windows, each with their inevitable drape of vertical, textured louvres, I reflected on the conceit that espionage might really be motivated by a hatred of such office environments, and the consequent need to 'get out into the field'.

Tony Blair's government may be hanging fire as far as greater *glasnost* is concerned, but surely it wouldn't be too much hassle to move MI6 into somewhere a little less banal? Oh, and they could put a nameplate on it as well.

WAPPING LIES

If there has been one constant throughout 20 years of political flux in this country, it has been the persistence with which *bien-pensant* liberals have 'loathed' Rupert Murdoch, News International, and everything else to which the Dirty Digger (a.k.a. The Dark Prince) has turned his attention. I place loathed in quotes because while it's true that the aforementioned canape-cutters profess to hate the man, they are, of course, perfectly prepared to buy his newspapers, and if, by any chance, they happen to be journalists, work for them.

Really, in the wake of the victory of an air-guitar-playing, Genesis-listening premier, whose party received a ringing endorsement from all the 666 organs of the Beast, it's difficult to keep one's loathing in any kind of shape at all. Either we must hate anybody who owns a newspaper in this country – the option I prefer – or else we're in danger of going belly-up to a toxic relativism.

In order to stiffen my resolve I decided to take a trip down to Wapping and sample the atmosphere. I was particularly intrigued to find out whether the epithet 'fortress' still applies to this redoubt of the establishment media, owned by an iconoclastic, naturalised American, Australian, hereditary newspaper magnate.

Rumbling in the motor-tumbril over Tower Bridge I apprehended the real reason why Wapping, rather than any other strike zone, should have been dubbed a fortress – its proximity to the Tower of London. Although the Tower, now cemented into modernity by the sub-urbanity of wood-mullioned windows, is far less threatening than any of the mirrored towers which dominate the City of London.

On the north bank I turned right along Wapping High Street and found myself utterly hemmed in by tedious office blocks to the left, and a high concrete rampart to the right. After 200 yards I turned into Artichoke Hill, and parked the car on cobblestones, next to a derelict building, and opposite the 50-foot, ancient brick wall that bounds the fiefdom.

The compound includes a number of buildings, old and new. Three concrete-and-smoked-glass, medium-rise blocks dominate the compound. As if this were some paradoxical, inner-city industrial estate, these blocks even have their own patch of open ground, complete with picnic area. But running along the wall where I parked is the much older, low-rise building which houses *The Times*; and across the way are the modern, barn-like structures which bellow and roar with the activity of the feared presses.

It wasn't that much like entering a fortress either. The security was only mildly more stringent than other newspapers – a bag search and a revolving security gate made out of perspex.

My informant worked on *The Times*. 'This building', he told me, 'was built by prisoners during the Napoleonic wars. We've been here for a while, but the windowlessness gets people down, so we're moving across the road …'. In fact, to a modern, glassy building called La Lumière, outside the fortress gates. I wonder, could this betoken some further, messier 'liberalisation' of the press? How loathsome.

BRIDGING THE EXPLODED METAPHOR

There are plenty of hackneyed turns of phrase in English that borrow from the architectural: finding keystones, laying foundations, and – most inapposite this one – building bridges. As any fool knows, there's nothing intrinsically good about building a bridge. (By this, I don't mean to suspend above you an argument which takes this figure of speech metaphorically – I mean just that.) John Augustus Roebling (1806–1869) could tell us all a thing or two about why this should be so. Roebling devised the first suspension bridges built using air-strung wire rope. A German, he attended Berlin Polytechnic and then went to America, where he founded a wire-rope factory near Pittsburgh. He built the long-span wire suspension bridge at Niagra Falls, and even though it worked he was still laughed at.

Nevertheless, it was his design that won the competition for a bridge across the Hudson joining Manhattan and Brooklyn. The men who built that bridge had to go under the river in massive caissons with roofs of pine 30-feet thick. The caissons were the size of two football pitches, and the air they had to breathe was pushed down from the surface by primitive pumps. It had never been done before, and naturally enough the workmen got the bends (which was named 'caisson disease' – some etiology!), and died in droves. Tell it to them about the value of building bridges.

But it isn't the sheer cost of human life that's exercising me so much today, as the amount of human self-deception involved in positive bridge building. There's one advert on the box at the moment which – figuratively speaking – makes me feel as if someone has treated my scrotum as the propellor of a model aircraft. It's advertising yet another two-millimetre-thick shell of powered silver steel; another corporate vehicle doomed to either spend its working life unsold in a gargantuan car park, or barely used in the giant tailbacks that constitute what is laughably called our 'road system'.

I can't, thankfully, remember much about the ad – or perhaps I've repressed it – but it does involve bridges. Impossible bridges. The silver pod powers towards the edge of a mighty, yet virtual, Grand Canyon, but before it can plunge over the edge these bridges shoot out from the lip of the gulch. They are heroic constructions, cleverly underpinned by what appear to be extendable props. The bridges are also a Promethean silver, and couldn't possibly exist in this form; even in the best of all possible worlds.

Indeed, every time I see the ad I think to myself what a cheesy, yet philosophically sound, portrait it is of any automotive future as far as the built environment is concerned. In order for a motorist in Britain's built-up areas to feel ease of movement, in this coagulated day and age, it would be essential for her car to be able to project from its front end a stream of solid, durable, yet completely individual flyover. A kind of car ectoplasm – as if the driver were a high-speed, spiritualist medium.

And dare I say that this ad does work also at a metaphoric level. The perverse adherents of the road lobby continue to behave as if we could go on and on building massive flyovers until the whole country looks like a set from Fritz Lang's *Metropolis*. This week, in the wake of John Prescott's White Paper on transport, voices are already being raised deploring the threat to Britain's drivers. The two-Volvo SIPSocracy ('my kids live – yours die') of Middle England. 'Privatisation,' mouthed one of these idiots, 'is the only solution to the current situation.'

Once and for all: the law – as De Toqueville so justly observed – exists to restrain our worst impulses, not to encourage our best. It exists to prevent us driving across virtual Grand Canyons on impossible bridges, not encourage us to go white-water rafting.

There are some professionals who have a more proactive role to play in all of this. You for starters. Until architects are prepared to make a principled stand against contributing to the current autogeddon, not only in terms of roads and their infrastructure, but also by declining to design buildings which in and of themselves depend on the car for their *raison d'être*, the current choking, snarling imbroglio will continue as it is – but worse.

I'm as much to blame as the rest of us. I drive a large three-litre saloon without a catalytic converter. But increasingly I feel when driving as if I might as well be sitting at home injecting lead directly into the brains of my children. So restrain me Mr Prescott, please do, but don't moralise – it doesn't suit you.

SICKENING BUILDINGS

So, whatever scepticism remained in our dear leader's sainted brow concerning the Millennium Dome has now evaporated, like some dew of uncertainty burnt off by the hot sun of reason. As Lewis Carroll has written: 'O frabjous day! Callooh! Callay!'

I wonder – purely in passing – whether our leader's attitude towards other monumental British buildings has undergone a similar conversion experience. I like to imagine him waking up at dawn, quitting No. 11, and taking a Wordsworthian stroll across Westminster Bridge. Instead of allowing his keen, metaphoric mind to focus and flirt with the ruckled, glaucous surface of the Thames, I like to picture him transfixed by the beauty of St Thomas' Hospital.

Yes, Tone would think, this isn't a building that should stand for only a few years, it should endure into the next millennium, a potent symbol of … what exactly? In a very important sense, in our culture, the hospital is the primal structure, the architectural alpha and omega. It is both our womb and our grave, a giant petri dish full of life-sustaining technology and, increasingly, life-destructive super viruses. It would be a cosmic irony if, in some far distant future, a Sir Edward Carstairs-type archeologist were to succumb to the mummy's curse when excavating a long-buried maternity hospital.

I was born in the old Charing Cross Hospital, which no longer exists – or rather it's been relocated right across London to the Fulham Road, where its sub-Bauhausian irrationality appears subject to more than the usual depredations of under-funding.

That's the thing about hospitals. In the absence of an ecclesiastical architecture that either operates from the top down – imposing an arcane architectonic on the people from above – or expresses the core spirituality of the people in vernacular terms (one thinks of the superb, carved angel ceiling at Blythburgh Church in Suffolk), it is left to the hospitals to express the relationship between eschatology and the built environment.

And what a messy business it is. The architects of modern hospitals may set out, with the best will in the world, to reconcile form and function, only to find that their work is consistently suborned, altered and undermined – even as it's undertaken. Provision must be made for extra wards here; a new kind of laboratory needs to be built over there, and in the meantime the funds necessary to sustain this particular clinic have quite simply disappeared.

No wonder that the experience of walking around most large modern hospitals is so profoundly disconcerting. Yes, there may well be electric doors activated by photocells – but they're defunct, so that the doors are wedged open with orange-plastic milk crates. The atrium is a fine idea, introducing a well of space and light into what might otherwise be a diseased termite heap. But it's no help at all that the atrium is overgrown with weeds and features a Brancusi-style bronze which some imitator knocked off while providing a stool sample.

The ranks of escalators suggest a speedy, efficient rise to

the different departments of this health store, yet inevitably they're out of order. And when you gain the upper storeys you find yourself wandering at first through abandoned wards with stripped bedsteads, and then through barely functioning wards where the patients are tethered by life-supporting shackles. Naturally, there is no one to blame for any of this, hospitals must always be built in a spirit of optimism, there's little point in setting out purposively to build a necropolis – unless you're a Parsee, that is.

Nonetheless, what strikes me most when I visit hospitals – and I do it no more nor less that anyone else – is the way the ebb and flow of funding and the restructuring of fiscal administration is organically expressed by the buildings themselves. The solution to the closure of this department and the establishment of that lab is to transform the structure into a mucilage of little units. Nowadays almost every major hospital is surrounded by its own *favela,* or shanty town, of Portakabins.

I'm not going to make a great stink about this, I understand all too well the pressure everyone concerned is under: the determination of the tax-paying public to have complete and free palliation of everything that ails them. But still, I can't help feeling that a truly attractive, integrated hospital might well go some way to inspiring the patient with confidence.

In the meanwhile, with their John Menzies franchises, cash points and coffee shops, the big hospitals increasingly resemble air terminals for the dying.

'Unaccustomed ...'

FANNY RUNS FROM CONGRESS

In Fiona MacCarthy's remarkable memoir of the celebrated smock-wearer Eric Gill,* much is made of his more exotic sexual practises (that's a euphemism for hopeless perversions, though why I bother I don't know), including having congress with his dog, Fanny. I have a lot of problems with this – I've only ever encountered one dog who could conceivably have had sufficient maturity and insight to engage in a consensual sexual act, and he was in the cabinet.

Gill was remarkable for other things as well – not least of which are the typefaces which bear his name. Listen, I have unbounded admiration for the art of architecture; tremendous enthusiasm for painting; enormous respect for the plastic arts; but when it comes right down to it the embodiment of *techne* that I admire the most has to be typography. There is something utterly pure about designing a series of beautiful and coherent shapes which are also the very essence of expression, the medium through which all intelligence is communicated.

Gill was a dab hand at stone carving as well. He was one of the few among his contemporaries – if not the only – who could carve directly, freehand, into stone.

Remarkable; it's as if a bricklayer were to buy a plot, and

* *Eric Gill*, Faber & Faber 1990.

then without so much as a few preliminary sketches on the back of an envelope, set to work constructing a house.

I digress; the reason Gill was on my mind was that his infamous bas-reliefs on the façade of Broadcasting House were the last thing I glimpsed through the back window of the minicab, as I sped away in the direction of the Design Museum. My destination was the Young Architect of the Year Awards, sponsored by British Steel (not yet an oxymoron), and organised under the auspices of *Building Design*, our own dear organ. (That almost sounds as obscene as Gill's goings on.)

I'd been at the BBC to record a short interview for a new series that's being put together on the aesthete through the ages, so the Gill carvings led to the smock-wearing, which in turn led to my keen anticipation of the forthcoming awards do. What would the well-dressed architecturati be wearing? Would they port accessories or not? In short, what would be the general tenor of the gathering?

In some ways it was a nice irony that the awards were presented at the Design Museum, the brainchild of Stephen Bayley, a deliriously amusing and caustic critic of the Blair regime's attempts to employ design and architecture as just two more modes within which to deploy their presentation skills; skills the regime seems intent on substituting for any substantive policies on the built environment. Nice irony, because the entirely amiable Nigel Coates – the government's favourite constructor of the moment – was on the jury for the prize; as was the still more amiable Norman Foster.

I remember when the museum was first built, and stood, marooned in among a broken terrain of rundown wharves

and derelict warehouses. Now it has been entirely surrounded by what – for want of any less inflammatory term
– I can only describe as the Conran ghetto. I said as much
during my little speech while I was opening the golden
envelopes containing the winners' names (hand-crafted by
the entire board of Pentagram), and then passing over the
cheques (layout and computer typography courtesy of
Neville Brody). It didn't seem that implausible to imagine
an extreme, anti-aesthetic junta of the future – after all,
there have been plenty in the past – herding anyone in the
country who has the temerity to embrace style in all its
manifestations, into this confined section of the Thames
littoral.

I didn't enlarge on this idea at the ceremony, but I can
imagine it all too well: being forced to eat expensive Conran groceries and sleep on the cobblestone streets; or else
offer one's sexual favours to the *maître d'* at The Chop
House, in return for being allowed to catch a couple of
hours sleep with your head down on the bar.

There was a goodly crowd out for the ceremony, and by
golly they were smartly turned out – and replete with
accessories. I knew I shouldn't have worn my smock.

HIDEOUS ATRIUM

And entirely so, for it's that point, on the cusp of winter, when I become convinced that the science-fiction fantasies of my childhood (usually promulgated in the form of back-of-the-cereal-packet panegyrics to a technologically fabulous late twentieth century), have indeed come to pass. The entire metropolis has been surmounted – and not just poor old, choking Greenwich – in an enormous translucent dome. The city feels intensely claustrophobic, like a room in which nobody has troubled to do the washing up for a couple of millennia, and I'm incapable of leaving it. So this isn't just a week spent *within* the built environment, it's a week entirely *bricked up* in the cellar of urbanity.

TUESDAY
File column for *Building Design*, then drive down through the Elephant and Bermondsey to have lunch with Gill Morgan, the editor of *The Times Magazine*, at the Blueprint Café in the Design Museum. The Museum seems a tad passé now; sandwiched between the trendy movie lot of Conran City and still-burgeoning apartment developments. There used to be a perfectly decent vacant lot next to it, where you could park for three quid. No more. Now you have to tip the commissionaire three quid when you

take the lift up to your loft.

The café itself is fairly thinly occupied – can the recession be already biting into fashionable biting? From the jumble of buildings on the north side of the Thames I single one out for scrutiny. It's bulky, double-arched, somewhere between a railway terminus and a mock-castle. 'D'you know what that is?' I ask Gill. She looks bemused: 'Err, it's News International Will.'

'It's not too bad from this angle really.'

'I think those towers could do with being bigger', she says and stabs her stacked cuisine. I goggle: News International bigger? Now there's a thought.

WEDNESDAY

Stay in and work. Keep the blind down. Built environment reduced to the architectonics of mind and desk. Occasionally deploy 030 scale models of American astronauts in small groups about the desktop – in order to give myself the sense of conquering new worlds.

THURSDAY

On the way to lunch with the estimable Louise Rogers (editor of *Building Design*), I muse again on the crappy, sub-Richard Rogers bits of glass canopy and tiling that have been glued on to the Oval tube station. This has always been an uncompromisingly gloomy and dour part of London -- why ruin things now?

After lunch I head on to the Grosvenor Hotel at Victoria to meet with an expert on weapons. This is an entirely apt venue. When I was a child this north side of the station was impressive beyond belief: as well as the hotel (which, even as a kid, I was aware actually formed the wall of the station, thus simultaneously compromising and formulating the integrity of the larger structure), there was the non-stop cartoon cinema, which stood, a pillar of mirth, next to the cab entrance. In through the cab entrance flew fog and pigeons, which disappeared among the stygian iron girders overhead. Now, of course, all this has changed and Victoria has, as it were, been fully encapsulated. So much so that there's an entire business centre within it – now that's progress.

Fortunately, although the Grosvenor has also been Thistle-ised, there's really not that much that can be done to compromise the massiveness of J Knowles's 1861 heap of Bath stone. The acres of burgundy carpet, and interior walls clad with marble, are resistant to the tramp of the centuries. This is still somewhere you'd unhesitatingly choose to make a dubious assignation.

FRIDAY
Went on *Newsnight* to discuss class and was insulted by some ludicrous epigone. I, unfortunately, was unable to pay any attention, because I was thinking about three other things that were far more important:
1 What a strange similarity Television Centre bears to the peculiar nature of the BBC itself; with its crazy ramming together of futurism and the past.
2 Kirsty Wark's fascinating ears.
3 The panorama of London that sits behind the programme's interviewees is a large piece of cloth with a slide of London back-projected on to it. How like life.

SATURDAY
Gave a reading at the Old Truman Brewery on Brick Lane. Vast gaff, almost entirely empty save for a few young face-

metal wearers slumped on sag-bags. Afterwards get a tad inebriated with Phil Dirtbox and others. We end up sitting in the new atrium which has been stitched on to the front of the building: acres of oppressive red brick. I find myself muttering under my breath: 'Hideous atrium, hideous atrium ...' until Phil observes that this would make a good short story. Or *Building Design* column for that matter.

'I suppose you have to expect your house to be in the vernacular, if your architect is a bear with very little brain ...'

THE BEST DAYS OF YOUR LIFE

When I interviewed Zaha Hadid for the *Independent on Sunday*, I felt compelled to round off my portrait by visiting her atelier. Not that the Great Woman would be in attendance herself, but there were plenty of epicene acolytes on hand to run their hands over Zaha's sinuous curves.

In truth, what most struck me about the atelier was that it was housed in an old elementary school with separate gendered entrances: snot-coloured rendering forming two vague bas-reliefs for 'boys' and 'girls'. I wondered at the time whether Zaha's boys and girls ever felt that their lives had somewhat stalled as they filed into work each morning.

It has to be analogous to the position of the person who coined the slogan, 'Today is the First Day of the Rest of your Life'. Let alone the stress and futility which must surely be engendered in this individual by seeing the fruits of her glib creativity plastered on bumpers and badges and stickers; there must also be the raw angst summoned up by the dawning revelation, that yes, this is indeed the first day of the rest of her life, but that it changes nothing.

I'm still very much in 'back to school' mode, as you can no doubt tell from the above. Indeed, I managed to usher my school-age duo back into the arms of Mother State only this morning. Some people imagine that writers must be highly disciplined individuals, but the truth of the matter is that we're highly suggestible. We don't need the threatening boss/teacher standing over us because we've already internalised this figure. 'Please sir, the dog ate my novel' is an excuse which often occurs to me.

This week sees the launch of the *Building Design/* British Steel Young Architect of the Year Award, and I note from the invitation that I'm scheduled to appear at the RIBA alongside various luminaries to debate the question: 'Are young architects getting the breaks they deserve?' In my mind this should really read: 'Are young architects breaking the gits who deserve it?', because the truth of the matter is I haven't a clue. I feel paralysed by ignorance in this field – as I do in so many.

I didn't think I was going to be able to file a column today at all, until I received in the mail a lushly expensive promotional pack for St Martin's Lane, the new Ian Schrager hotel opening this very day in London's Covent Garden. Even the keenest youth hostellers among you will be aware of Schrager's status as the *hotelier de nos jours*, the creator of such palaces of repose as the Royalton in New York, the Mondrian in LA, and the Delano in Miami. I have been known to nearly put my eye out on some modernist interior-design feature, while drunkenly staggering to my bed in one of these gaffs.

The promotional pack consists of no less than seven lushly executed pen-and-wash drawings of the new Schrager hotel. I have to say that they do remarkably little for me, though the one depicting the 'sea bar' is teasingly surreal, suggesting that the guests have the opportunity to operate an oceanic computer, with lobsters and mussels in lieu of a more conventional keyboard. No, the reason I remark upon it is that to stay in a hotel in the city in which you actually live has to be one of the most existentially queasy experiences you can have.

I once stayed the night in Claridge's (for an article – yeah, you guessed), and was appalled by the ants'-nest view it afforded me of the whole of my life. From the vantage point of an hotel room in central London all of my socio-cultural, political and economic definers became grotesquely salient: it was the Naked Lunch and I could see what was writhing on the end of my fork. I wonder how many young architects have made a point of sleeping the night in the first building which they completed during their career? It seems self-evident that the effects on the unconscious would be, to say the least, pronounced. And when they awoke in the morning and struggled to get dressed amid the lumber of reveries, I'm sure they'd be in little doubt that this particular morning was the first day of the rest of their career.

MINTING IT

'I think I feel one of your *Building Design* columns coming on', said my wife, with a broad grin on her face as Family Self trooped across the courtyard towards the Waterloo barracks. 'I don't know why,' she continued 'but for some reason this place makes me feel very happy.'

It certainly was bizarre. There's nothing that ostensibly jolly about the Tower of London. Indeed, in its unpoetic composition of towers and courtyards, one can see written all the hideous acts of violence that constituted rule by unconstitutional monarchy. As surely as Auschwitz or Belsen carry in their mechanised lineaments the hideous implication of assembly-line death; so the Tower, with its huddles of cottagey dwellings here, and its outcrops of militaristic knapping over there, presents the sustained narrative of death as a very domestic affair.

Yup, this is a little Kremlin of a joint, in which were you, for example, a Plantagenet, you might breakfast heartily in the Lanthorn Tower, have a stroll on the south wall and then brace yourself for chapel with a couple of quick beheadings in the lea of the Beauchamp Tower. Obviously, these would be rather bijoux affairs, the main business of executions having been carried out on Tower Hill, where there was better accommodation for the unruly fans.

But the very substance of the Tower was to project the traditional basis of the English monarchy: might is right.

So the fact that it's developed in such an arrestingly piece-meal fashion: enlargement as a species of infill – all the way down from the original construction of the eleventh-century bastion on the remains of the Roman; to the Victorian terrace stashed under the east wall of the outer ward – only serves to emphasise the arbitrariness of our existing polity.

We dragged the kids through the medieval palace where we all marvelled at the gargantuan tables, lecterns and chests. Clearly, a major part of being mighty in those days was having furniture that was mighty difficult to shift. Our sense of being profoundly dissociated from our own nation's past was dramatised by the way we talked loudly, confident that none of the thousands surrounding us were likely to speak English that well (i.e. well enough to understand our family idiolect).

Furthermore, of the five of us, only I had ever visited the Tower before. I must have been around seven, and I remember little of it save for the obvious. I recall being shoved along in a pack of heaving bodies, which eventually thrust me into the presence of the crown jewels. It was like partaking in a religious ritual.

Nowadays the mustering of the unruly herd of foreign suppliants is managed far more industrially. On entering the Waterloo barracks (an unholy, castellated, mid nineteenth-century waterworks of a building), the touristic effluvia is channeled through a series of chutes. In the first room you can pass back and forth several times in front of a display of monarchical coats of arms; in the second three enormous video screens play footage of Elizabeth Windsor's coronation. In the third room you confront the baubles themselves in a novel fashion: two moving walkways (or 'flat escalators', as I still can't help thinking of them) transport you the 80-odd feet required to view the jewel-encrusted hats, sticks, spoons and balls. You may walk back to the beginning if you choose, but you will only ever be able to encounter the Koh-i-Noor diamond at two miles per hour or more.

If I were the marvellous, modernising Brer Blair I'd get rid of all this anachronistic rock worship and put the jewels in the British Museum, where they'd make up for the gap left by the return of the Elgin Marbles. Alternatively he could hand the Tower over to Brer Straw who could employ it in a traditional fashion. A place of confinement for high-profile child killers and abusers would be in the spirit of the place; strongly emphasising the notion of governance in opposition to a baying, immoral mob.

The one thing that shouldn't be continued is the crown's stewardship. At £30 a visit for a family (inclusive of official guide book), it has to be well out of range for a lot of ordinary British people. I really resent the monarchy coining it in this fashion – especially since they have a mint of their own anyway.

'Run for it! It's Mrs Harris!'

NOT TO SCALE

One of my main preoccupations as a writer of Surrealist fiction is the conundrum that the very notion of scale presents us with – time and time again. It's also provided me with a back passage into thinking about architecture; for I certainly never noticed the front door.

There seem to me to be several different complexes or gestalts bound up in the notion of scale. Firstly, we have our entire sense of the world radically and speedily transformed by the alterations in scale which is growing up; secondly, we inhabit an environment where mechanisation has altered our basic, ergonomic relations; and thirdly, we live in an allegedly 'globalised' society, throughout which personal bonds are becoming increasingly attenuated.

My wife sees the issue as far, far simpler. Initially she put the whole thing down to my height. While, at 6 foot 5 inches, I fall an inch short of official giganticism, I have nonetheless spent a lot of my adult life head-butting the architrave. But when she saw the chapel at Lancing College, Sussex, where there's an effigy of my great-great-grandfather, Nathaniel Woodard, she began to say that the whole thing was hereditary. Woodard, who founded Lancing among a slew of other public schools, got carried away with the chapel. While the rest of the school is a conventional enough hilltop huddle of stone buildings, the chapel – which thrusts out on a spur – has a nave bigger than

Notre Dame's. What a grandiose nutter.

But I think any preoccupation with scale remains, intrinsically, a philosophic problem. Particularly now when it seems to have become architecture's business to fundamentally distort and cheat our sense of scale. In the past the built environment was still either dependent on – or retained echoes of – a scale derived from the natural world, whether the mean was human or topographical. Even the Pantagruelian pyramids of the Pharaohs were a just expression of the sheer scale of a mundane deity. In the modern city the scale of buildings is often defined solely in relation to each other. People, animals, trees and cars can be peculiarly irrelevant to the aesthetic concerns of designers, who must, quite reasonably, seek to further harmonise the existing overall structure.

Bizarrely, I believe this tendency is transposed into other platforms of virtuality. In the week where Bill Gates concluded a deal with Britain's ICL for a series of new 'communications kiosks' to be built in our high streets, allowing for electronic access to goods and services of all kinds, I have found myself pondering the scaled-down phenomenon of computer architecture.

Gates's Windows software platform – the name itself is revealing – is based on the WYSIWYG (What You See Is What You Get) design pioneered originally by Macintosh. It hardly bothers with a third dimension – except in the rapid dissolves – configuring the visual display as a series of paper sheets which can be tiled. But even my machine, resolutely un-CAD, betrays other architectural features. The hardware itself reposes on my desktop like a miniature bypass-bound office development. The mini-tower is, of course, self evident, but even the VDU crouches at a rake suggestive of ramps and walkways; and its back and sides are indented with graticules of what might as well be more … well … windows.

I only have to write this gubbins, but I wouldn't fancy being an architect who was generating a three- or even four-dimensional model, on a machine which itself embodies a scaling down of the built environment. I mean *reductio ad absurdem* or what?! Especially if the virtual building remains just that: one putative form embodied in another digitised one.

Is it too fanciful to imagine that the superficial similarities we witness between objects designed and built for very different functions are, in terms of human, social evolution, a result of a particular – and putatively sinister – convergence? Or that the reason things look the same, no matter what their scale, is because scale itself is no longer relevant?

Believe me, I don't relish throwing up these questions, they come unbidden. And I certainly don't wish to leave you in the lurch, but the harsh facts of the matter are these, I need to print this piece out now and that involves some pretty lengthy trips – even if it is my fingers that are doing the walking.

BABYLON

The shaven-headed translator (who only translates from Dutch to German), with a chunky silver earring and a hacking jacket, puffs expansively on one of my Toscanelli cheroots, leans against the coffee bar of the Bouvier bookshop in Bonn and begins to expatiate on the aesthetics of Cologne. 'Actually, I think you will find Köln a very ugly city,' he is deep in a forest of Teutonic gloom. 'After the war they had no proper zoning – you know 70 per cent of the city was damaged by bombing; and I think people built pretty much how they wanted to, with no order.'

I may well find Cologne a very ugly city, but it can have nothing of the negative impact on me that Berlin did. I landed at Tiegel Airport and was gripped immediately by my own kind of Nordic dolour. It was cold – much colder than London; and, as I drove into town with Francesca Spinazzi, the organiser of the Berlin Festival (my reason for being there), I was struck by the proliferation of cranes, even since I'd last been here 18 months ago.

Bonn having been finally demoted from its position as a governmental centre, Berlin is flexing the muscles of its built environment as it girds up for capital calisthenics. Norman Foster's naked and cranial dome for the Riechstag is in place; and the futuristic planes of the new parliament building are beginning to assemble themselves.

('Too big! Too futuristic!' exclaimed Francesca Spinazzi.)

I'd chosen to arrive on the day of the reopening of the Potsdamerplatz. This area, athwart the old dividing line between East and West Berlin, has been designated the new cultural centre of Berlin. But although the streets were thronged with people, as yet there seemed no coherence to this pile of freshly poured concrete.

Here was the impressive home of the Berlin Philarmonic; next to Mies Van Der Rohe's art gallery; next to a mushroom outcropping of tapering concrete spires, blazoned with the corporate dark stars of the Far East: Sony, Fijutsu, Mitsubishi. In between the buildings twisted humped boulevards, masked off by hoardings, behind which cranes dipped their iron bills.

I daresay people who knew the old Berlin (or Berlins – there have been so many this century alone) may not regret its passing, but it is bizarre to see that Checkpoint Charlie has become another tract of anonymous banking boulevard. Still, this building frenzy cannot altogether obliterate the past. As we bumped across the 'platz, Francesca Spinazzi pointed out to me the neoclassical façade of Goering's old ministry; a chilly ghost at the expansionist feast.

I was put up in a venerable hotel – the Akanischer – on Kurfurstendamm. My room had a 25-foot ceiling and glass doors opening on to a glassed-in balcony. The bed, replete with oval headboard, was adrift in a quarter acre of space. The wallpaper, the furniture, the fittings – all were somehow German in their essence. This is, of course, what people really mean by culture shock: the automatic response to a comprehensive shift in the built environment which surrounds them.

In the afternoon we visited an exhibition of computer-generated animation put on by Herbert Fritzsch. One of the pieces was entitled *Building the Tower of Babylon*, and featured a computer programme which endlessly 'built' a simulacrum of said tower. On screen our point of view revolved round ceaseless staircases and galleries, always ascending, and occasionally looking down the illimitable stairwell, while a digital counter marked off the storeys: 26,709 since the exhibition had begun.

It would be nice to tell you that this work was an ironic comment by Herr Fritzsch on the construction frenzy all around, but I don't think it was. He, like so many Berliners I met, was entirely caught up in the *Zeitgeist*. They really seem to feel that the world spirit of urbanity has alighted on Berlin; and that this time it will stay.

It was a relief to get to Bonn, ruefully contemplating its demotion and scaling down to become the sleepy little university town it always was. But my shaven-headed informant was entirely wrong about Cologne. Ugly it may be – but what a majesty of ugliness! This is a city that's taken ugliness to new heights. A great mashing together of conflicting and gibing styles, materials, and proportions, all of it presided over by the cathedral. And what a cathedral! The Cathedral of the Magi is, like St Stephen's in Vienna, a carious victim of pollution-on-limestone. Its twin spires are calcified with blackness; vast lattice works lifting up into the grey sky, and buttressed with the scaffolds used for near endless restoration. Gothic doesn't get much higher.

But the best thing about the cathedral is that as you emerge from the Hauptbahnhof – a bog-standard piece of 1960s ugliness – you realise that the high, glassed-in entrance hall has been perfectly designed to frame the flank of the cathedral. As you move forward each successive glass panel reveals another piercing finial or soaring buttress. It may be a case of the dour framing the dourer, but it has to be one of the most exhilarating architectural experiences I've ever had.

Now I'm ensconced in the Hotel Hopper (named, the receptionist told me, after both Edward and Dennis), amid interior design so minimal it makes Philippe Starck look like Bernini. I may be some time here in Cologne.

'Completed on time! To budget! And it houses the finest billiard-cue collection in the world!'

THE SOLID MANDALA

In the week beginning the sixteenth of August 1999, spare a thought for David Marks and his partner Julia Barfield. While most of you will have little of architectural import on your minds save whether a shingle buttress will support a sand wall, Marks and Barfield will be facing 30 of the most crucial seconds ever in their professional lives. For, at some point during this week, when the wind is right, the tide is right, and the eclipse-crazed mobs of moonheads have been canalised by the constabulary, a stupendously huge crane sited at Victory Gardens on London's South Bank, will take up the strain and attempt to lift all 20,000-odd tons of the world's biggest-ever Ferris wheel into an upright position.

When Marks, who was showing me over the Millennium Eye site the other day, let fall this tensile intelligence, I forbore from remarking that if things did go wrong, it would at least be the biggest splash made in the capital for a very long time. Nor did I make some snide crack about rolling 'one toke over the line', when Marks proudly displayed to me what must surely be the biggest joint London has ever seen; a plug of specially smelted stainless steel which will, we all hope, ensure that the big wheel keeps on turning.

No, I was altogether captivated by Marks, a quintessential tall guy with sparkling blue eyes, who when I encoun-

tered him was struggling manfully to deal with a gargantuan charge of adrenalin. He and Barfield (who's his personal as well as professional partner) thought of the wheel
in response to a newspaper-sponsored competition for
commemorative millennial structures held some six years
ago. Eschewing lottery money, they went for city backing
and corporate sponsorship. I think the wheel is so good
that the government should've stumped up for it. There's a
grand tradition of social security and Ferris wheels, as
Marks himself was able to inform me.

Apparently, the 200-foot-high Ferris wheel which
used to revolve in Earl's Court at the turn of the century
was so vulnerable to the wind, that punters were dobbed a
sixpence if they got stuck on the thing. Locals would board
the wheel on a regular basis, confident of their arresting
stipend. Now, poor Marks and Barfield and Bob Ayling
and a couple of City banks and Uncle Tom Cobbly and all
the rest of the Millennium Eye's investors, have to hope
not just that the thing gets upright, but that it will keep
right on revolving the six years their lease allows for, all
that time carting some tens of millions of paying souls
around its humungous hub. Otherwise they're all going to
be severely out of pocket. Not that wind is going to be a
problem – they've got that sorted out. There are damper
systems; the cars (or rather capsules) are gyroscopically
mounted and independently powered; the Eye also has its
own electricity substation, and so on.

I'm quite confident that the Eye will break even, but I
don't want poor David Marks to have to worry about it,
he has enough bearing down on him as it is. However, I'm
not so sure I agree with him when he says he wants the
Eye, after its residency on the South Bank, to become 'like

the Crystal Palace'. I mean, I don't think there's much virtue in the thing being carted off to Sydenham for the next 80-odd years before having it burn down in an enormous fire.

No, I must admit I did tease its poor creator to this extent. I suggested that just possibly, in those odd peripheral moments, while swimming in the grey, amniotic haze that joins sleep to wakefulness, he might be entertaining – merely entertaining – the very remotest possibility of changing his name to David Eiffel. He blushed – a difficult thing to do for one such as himself, weathered by the gritty winds of the Thames estuary, and denied any such claim upon posterity.

I was only kidding, of course. But I'm not sure I wouldn't like the Eye to remain longer than its allotted time, given that David Marks and his craning cohorts can get it up to begin with. I'm always belabouring the point that it's senseless spending time constructing a built environment which cannot be seen. The Eye will give us the finest viewing platform the capital has ever witnessed. Never before have we had quite so long – 25 miles – or so central a perspective. It will give us the urban equivalent of being a cat catching sight of its own tail in a mirror. Fade in the creepily elegiac zither music – and keep it cranked right up.

Brian Sewell criticises a radio mast in the Siberian tundra.

UNRIVALLED PROSPECTS

Arriving in Seattle there is much for the eye to take in: a majestic sweep of coastline; a fine plantation of proud skyscrapers; the egregious Boeing plant, complete with ominous, bulbous, military aircraft; and the petrified ticker-tape of flyovers and underpasses running this way and that. But turn on the local tourist information channel (this is, after all, America, and there's a channel dedicated to just about anything), and you find that the natives feel there's something special about their 'space needle'. This, the tallest building in town, is an inelegant parabola of concrete, sweeping up to support a disc-shaped module, which, naturally, revolves, giving unrivalled views of ... unrivalled views.

It's reminiscent of similar structures in Toronto, in Copenhagen, and in our own dear London. What is it that makes these intrinsically childish buildings objects of civic pride? They have all the architectural merit of a Squeezy bottle spray-painted silver. The Telecom Tower in London – formerly known as the Post Office Tower – had the dubious distinction of being bombed 30 years ago, putting paid to London's only revolving restaurant. It has to be said, this is the kind of direct action that could give terrorism a good name.

But barring some hideous, Oklahoma-style incident,

there's little possibility of that happening to the space needle. Instead, it will remain, pointlessly penetrating the sky, and providing the inspiration for a range of jewellery. I kid you not, I saw this stuff advertised. You can get space needle pendants, space needle earrings – indeed, just about any space needle bauble your heart desires.

In Britain this would be absurd enough – but in the US where all downtown areas are dominated by 40- and 50-storey towers, the special status accorded to a tower for being circular and non-functional, looks as superstitious and batty as a cargo cult. Yet American cities are topped-off with numerous such structures, many of which revolve so as to give you unrivalled prospects of … other tall buildings. In connection with this I remember one particularly grim evening I spent in Minneapolis, staying in a skyscraping hotel with a revolving restaurant. Come dinner time I was the only diner. The sight of the poor waitress, having to wait and time her descent from the stationary core, to the rotating periphery – where I sat, eating a steak the size of a cow – was enough to make you want to call up the building's owner and say: 'For God's sake man, just turn the thing off once in a while, and we can all get on with normal life.'

SNICE WORK

I hadn't been looking forward to my trip to the ICEHotel, which is at a place called Jukkas Jarvi, north of the Arctic Circle in Sweden. Cold and Self are not easy bedfellows and the hotel – which is built afresh out of ice and 'snice' (more of which later) each year – boasts below-freezing bedrooms.

The temperature hovers around minus four and you're meant to cuddle up in your sleeping bag and think boreal thoughts. The 'beds' you lie on are made of blocks of translucent ice; the furniture in the room is carved from ice; even the arty, Modernist candle bracket (if such an artefact is believable) is made from ice.

The ICEHotel is the dream child of a man called Ingve Bergqvist, who together with the architects Ake Larsson and Arne Berg have made it an impressive – if faintly pointless – reality. I stayed at the hotel – if not actually in it – for a couple of nights, and managed to grab a few words with Arne who, along with the rest of his team, was working flat out to finish the structure and all its appurtenances before the grand opening on 30 December. 'You see,' he exclaimed, gesturing at one of the main arches supporting the central hall of the hotel, 'we build the place out of these arches, but it's only possible to make them five metres high. If we make them six metres high they collapse.'

This is, of course, a function of the properties of the

aforementioned 'snice', the material which constitutes the bulk of the building. Snice is a half-and-half compound of snow and ice, all mixed up together and then applied, like cement, to a form. Once it's frozen in place the form is removed, repositioned next to it, and the process is repeated to create a series of nave-like and chancel-like, interconnecting vaults. The main vaults are the bar, the reception area etc., and the side vaults are further subdivided for the frigid bedrooms. Outside, in among the clutter you'd associate with any building site, there was a large machine pumping out a white gout of particulate spume. 'Snow machine,' my guide explained 'we haven't had enough yet this year.'

There is another structural component – the eponymous one. Beside the hotel is a mighty river which throughout the winter freezes to a deeper and deeper level, and it's from here that they quarry an astonishing, blueish, pellucid ice. Circular sections of this are stacked up to make the pillars which support the snice vaulting. Ice is also used to build large 'windows' at the end of vaults, through which light eerily percolates. Occasionally a tiny piece of weed or algae gets suspended in one of these blocks, enhancing the feeling that the building is elemental and organic, rather than fabricated.

Abutting the hotel are a series of auxiliary igloos which are used to mount art exhibitions. While I was there, a posse of Japanese ice sculptors was in residence and the site was full of pigtailed Japanese girls dragging blocks of ice round on tiny sleds, then stacking them into scintillating menhirs. There were also lighting artists and interior designers labouring to make the main structure into a colossal ice sculpture in its own right.

In order to prevent the thing becoming unstable while it's under construction, there's a network of pipes on the floor which contain saline water. These ensure that the temperature remains resolutely below freezing. I could see a few cracks in the snice, but they'd been grouted with still more of the same. Handy stuff.

There's no denying that the ICEHotel is a beautiful thing to contemplate – even though you wouldn't want to stay there. (Anyway, guests only sleep the night in the ice rooms, during the days they repair to well-insulated huts.) But just how much genuine architectural excellence it represents is moot. Arguably there's something intrinsically decadent about expending so much energy on an utterly ephemeral project. Mind you, the hotel's brought heaps of employment to Jukkas Jarvi. There's even a couple in the village who make a handsome living turning out 'ice glasses' for the hotel's Absolut Ice Bar. These they drill out from blocks of ice – cheap or what!

The basic utility of the ICEHotel didn't seem to bother any of these guys – they'd spent their summer supplying a contract ice structure for a fashion show. In Niger. As Raymond Chandler would've put it: it's difficult to imagine a greater waste of human time and ingenuity outside of an advertising agency.

HOMAGE TO THE BATHROOM

My trips to the States are increasingly formed and predicated on the wishes of my half-brother, the architectural historian, Professor Nick Adams. On this outing I managed to disappoint him mightily. Prior to departure there was a flurry of faxes suggesting that I dedicate my visit to the following: a rewriting of Baudrillard's *America;* followed by an interview with Philip Johnson; leading ultimately to my attendance at an important architectural conference in NYC featuring – among others – Peter Eisenman and Daniel Libeskind.

In the event I rocked up to his immaculate gaff in upstate New York and spent the next few days turning the duvet in his spare room into a sponge, as I twisted and turned in the vise of flu. It was the right place to shake, in among his small collection of Shaker furniture, but eventually I managed to regain my feet and head into town.

Before I left Nick managed one final injunction: 'While you're there, go and see Robert Irwin's installation in Chelsea; he's the grandfather of American conceptual art. It's really quite an amazing piece. Spend some time in there – it's simply a room, but he's done very interesting things to it. Believe me, stay for a while and you'll lose your sense of orientation, your sense of scale, and finally you'll begin to see ghosts.'

A tempting proposition – especially in a city which, for me, always feels freighted with the supernatural. Anyway, having failed his other injunctions I took my friend Zoë off to see 'Excursus: Homage to the Square 3'. We trooped leadenly through the leaden streets of midtown Manhattan. Between Broadway and Chelsea there was a mile or so of old brownstones; many of their interiors (we peeked in a lot) completely unaltered for many years. Ah! how the city doth tease with its incongruities!

Then we began running into small posses of Village types clustered around the brightly lit entrances to converted loft spaces, and we knew we'd arrived. If final confirmation was required it came in the form of a coach, which splashed us in passing, bearing on its side a placard reading: ART SHUTTLE.

At the Dia Centre, 548 West 22nd Street there was a goodly crowd of conceptual groupies queued up to see works by Joseph Beuys and Douglas Gordon (former Turner Prize contender), as well as the Irwin. Zoë needed the bathroom and was told it was on the third, the same floor as the Irwin exhibition. We ascended in a stainless steel lift and debouched straight into the middle of 'Excursus: Homage to the Square 3'. The whole width and breadth of the converted warehouse had been remodelled by Irwin to strange effect. In the bare space he'd fabricated a sequence of square spaces, each defined by sheets of moiré material running from floor to ceiling, these, in turn, were framed by low-intensity neon tubes.

The whole effect – with the moiré sheets running across the windows turning the already dark New York afternoon into something lunar – was Escher-like: the squares leading into one another in such a way as to suggest that they would go on *ad infinitem*, whilst the hip wandered among them, rendered insubstantial by framing. Yes, we were for a short while disorientated, but then we saw a big guy in a hooded blue top who was porting a two-way radio. He was standing in the corner of one of the squares, arms crossed, and lowering at the procession of existentialist inhabitants of the inner city, who came and went, talking not of Michelangelo. Wherever we moved inside the debatable boundaries of 'Excursus: Homage to the Square 3', we could still see the guy.

To quote from the catalogue copy: ' "Excursus: Homage to the Square 3" builds on this intense, phenomenologically based engagement, while shifting the focus subtly from the locus, the site in its widest sense, in order to create a more hermetic situation in which colour becomes the principal agent: light is now materialised hue.' Well, err … yeah, it would've been, save for the guy in the blue top, because wherever we went we couldn't escape sight of his hue; he was a still point in this fluxus. However hard we tried to lose ourselves in the installation, he kept looming up to remind us where we were. So, eventually, we asked him where the bathroom was.

SPACE 1999

I've seen more than my fair share of conceptual art, and it may surprise you to learn that in my unhumble opinion some of it is brilliant and some of it utter shite. Securely in the latter category was a travesty of a 'performance' which I attended with my long-suffering wife Deborah on 10 July 1999. Why has it taken you so long to write about this? I hear you ask. The answer is that it's taken me a month or so for my extreme anger with the perpetrators of this gross rip-off to subside.

It cost no less than 50 smackers for us to attend the 'art work' designated *Home 2*; and as we left during the interval (thank god there was one so we could) I told Deborah I'd be cancelling the cheque I'd written for the tickets first thing the following morning. I wish I had – but I suppose I didn't because I felt such an ass for attending *Home 2* in the first place. The idea behind *Home 2* was, according to the puff sheet, that: 'Public and private spaces collapse into each other, as specially staged pieces transform the kitchen, bathroom, bedroom, studio and office into a performance laboratory. Playing off the domestic surroundings, this company of performers, which includes some of Britain's foremost performance artists … will explore a variety of themes reflecting contemporary roles, obsessions and transformations in home life.' Hmm, put like that it could've been interesting.

But the reality was a couple of upper-middle-class twerps who'd turned their sub-designer house in Camberwell over to a bunch of grown-up children performing inadequate party turns. I'm as pretentious as they come, but this really stuck in my craw. On the invitation we were informed that *Home 2* is an arts trust; that it's sponsored by the Arts Council of England and that it 'subscribes to' *Everything* magazine. Along the bottom were corporate logos for: Half Time Based Arts; Kent Institute of Art and Design; *Make*, the magazine of women's art; the Nottingham Trent University; *Pink*; the Tower Printing Company Limited; and 291 Gallery.

It was unclear whether these institutions and companies were sponsoring *Home 2* or *vice versa*, but either way they should hang their collective head in shame for being associated with what, on the face of it, looked like a scam by a couple of bourgeois shysters to pay for their furnishings. The involvement of the Arts Council in particular led me to doubt that progressive taxation can be justified at all for very much longer.

The likes of Bobby Baker (who Deborah told me had been around since the year before dot), utilising two chairs, a table and a cool bag to present a send-up of dinner party preparation, might've been mildly satirical had it been presented in the context of a Royal Variety performance. But it led me to ponder anew what I've always suspected. Namely, that these kind of performers do what they do because they *can't* think, or write, or paint, or print; and that the audience pay to see them for the *same reason*.

While this farrago was underway the 'audience' sat in

the dining room of the house which unfortunately was a *Home* 2, either rapt, or photographing, or videotaping, or live telecasting to the net. Can you believe it? The real model for this sort of parlour entertainment is, of course, the posh salons of the nineteenth century. But whereas Proust's alter ego in *A La Recherche du Temps Perdu* would listen to the fresh pieces composed by a fictionalised Ravel; or scrutinise the paintings of a fictionalised Whistler, we were condemned to suffer the antics of real talentless no-hopers who should be forced to do raffia work and make clay pots in a specially constructed detention centre. We could call it *Camp* 2.

In fairness Joshua Sofaer – up to whose bed-based performance we all trooped after we were done in the dining room – did actually have some decent lines, and bar the odd bit of corpsing presented his turn with flair. I would've happily paid 50 pence to see him. But the final 'act' we witnessed was so pestilentially dull that I could feel the flies buzzing around my eyes as I struggled to remain upright. Lie down Gary Stevens, who far from presenting 'a new piece investigating the paradoxes of verbal description in a visible universe', simply intoned cod-surrealistic drivel and paced about.

But the real culprits are of course the owners of said *Home* 2, the self-styled 'artist' Laura Godfrey-Isaacs, and the 'structural designer' Glen Haddon. Where these two get off is beyond me. I wish I could be certain it was a calculated rip-off, but I fear they probably think they're doing something 'important'. People like that invariably do.

As we were running for the front door, Deborah said, 'I can't wait to get home.' 'Why?', I asked. 'Because it'll be a real home from Home.'

M

DEEP END

I've taken up swimming, and am now – like a character in Skolimowski's film *Deep End* – to be found floating, suggestively in this viscous municipal element, arms crossed behind my head, trunks casually unknotted, with an expression of Ortonesque sensuality playing across my rugged yet attractive features. I shan't be telling you which pool it is I bestow with my enpurpled form, because I don't want the water level to rise alarmingly as I am besieged by admirers prepared to plumb new depths.

Now, my swimming may be something of a head-down, no-nonsense breasting of the chlorine rather than a leisurely frolicking amid the mini-surf, but even so, every 25 metres the head comes up, the eyes revolve redly like the lights of the emergency services, and the architecture is taken in. There's no disputing the linkage between the public and the private baths; no way – even now, on the very cusp of the millennium – of decoupling the two. But even after a lengthy furlough away from the lengths, it astonishes me to find myself stripped naked inside a giant, and not particularly clean, bathroom. During the great Victorian age of municipal architecture, in which the public baths evolved, they were just that: baths, places where the working class could come and purchase H&C running, and a modicum of privacy.

So, on the interior the municipal baths architecturally converged with private bathrooms; while externally – through a feat of astonishing mimicry – they came to resemble public libraries. To continue the library decor inside the baths would have been a gross piece of misrepresentation: far better to warn the clientele that they are about to immerse themselves in a huge vat of little boys' urine, by making the interior of the baths look like any domestic toilet. I've heard tell, at late-night gatherings where I really shouldn't have been present, that some rotten boroughs actually purchase large quantities of little boys' urine from other boroughs, to make up their shortfall. You just can't be certain what you're swimming in nowadays.

In fairness to those charged with designing pools, it's only reasonable – given health and safety considerations – that large amounts of tiling should be employed. It's only proper that it should be little more than a giant splash-back, firmly grouted against the vicissitudes of the millrace of urban life.

Look at the problems pool designers get into when they attempt to break out of the bathroom. I've witnessed poolside murals at Rosscarberry in County Cork and the Metropole Hotel in Brighton which both attempt to give the swimmer the visuals she might have, were she to be foolhardy enough to try and bathe in the adjacent expanses of natural water, to whit: the Atlantic, and the Channel respectively. Using interior decoration to underscore the insalubriousness of our climes is hardly a selling point for a pool; but then nor are wave machines, potted palms, or any of the other pseudo–tropical gubbins designers install in an effort to make perfectly ordinary leisure centres look like a Centreparc. No, the only era of pool construction in

Britain which bears examination is the 1930s. The great lidos of this period made no concessions to either the notion of private space, or mimicry of some other country. These were the swimming pool as modern agora, where the citizen might stroll and disport himself, before picking up another citizen to go home and disport with.

I think the reason the lidos still appear so marvellously comfortable with their contexts – Saltdean Lido is the *ne plus ultra* – is that they were conceived in a spirit of genuine aspiration: people really wanted to swim there. Now, I really want to go swimming in the vat of little boys' pee up the road, but I think it's a prime candidate for a mural which reveals its surroundings to the panting porpoises within. That's right, what my local pool needs is a mural of the surrounding area on its interior walls. The high-rise blocks, the grinding traffic, the graffiti-bedizened bus shelters – let it all be faithfully depicted. Alternatively, just put some big windows in, and then we can all see what it is we're splashing around in.

RISING HACKLES OF URBANITY

Planners, potentates, princes, architects, building officers and local government officials of all stripes have had the hubris throughout this century and even during preceding ones to imagine that they can construct urban environments which will, if not exactly make people happy, still provide them with a suitable context within which to be born, procreate and then die.

Of course, that's not the way the people view it at all. Their sense of the world they inhabit is defined by a multiplicity of factors, of which the distance they have to walk to the shop, or the material construction of the bus shelter in which they have to wait is an empty category waiting to be filled by emotions, psyche, and aesthetics and then composted by memory. My mother had a favourite maxim: 'At least you can be miserable in good surroundings.' For the majority of modern urban dwellers who have suffered the depredations of planned built environments, this could easily be reversed: 'At least you can be good in miserable surroundings.'

Children grow into a sense of the world which is intimately connected with topography. This swims into vision, just as the child's sense of herself coalesces. Truly, at five or six we are all strangers in a brave new world of aching familiarity.

Last weekend I walked around my wife's childhood world – the housing estates, woods, and recreation grounds where she roamed as a girl. The place where there used to be a rope swing; the place where the tough kids lived; the place – in the grounds of the big house (now, of course, a series of luxury apartments) – where she discovered an overgrown Japanese garden; and the street she and her mother would walk down, fantasising that they lived in this or that house.

Then there were the buildings. The 17-storey blocks which stand along the ridge of the town – raised hackles of urbanity – are currently being clad in some kind of painted metal siding. All five of them. What a field day for tin men. The wheelhouses of the lifts are being encased in one-storey structures that most closely resemble a low-rent rip-off of the Chrysler Building. The blocks that have been finished look curiously Dutch (as do most British attempts to gild Modernism); the ones that are half finished – with the tracking for the new cladding already in place, splinting the broken concrete – are very *Blade Runner* indeed; while the ones yet to be clad have become timeless in their grey austerity. You wouldn't be at all surprised to see a small boy with a kestrel on his wrist wandering out of one of them.

As we traversed the area, my wife's talk was of alleyways and passages that had disappeared; woodland that had been eroded; and trash that had accumulated. This is a town which has always been regarded as fairly depressed, but through her eyes I began to see that in the 1960s these estates were pristine bits of futurist triumphalism.

But what impinged more was the overlap between her childhood environment and my own. I may have been brought up in the north London suburbs, but the area I ranged over was more or less the same extent: a rough oblong two miles by one. I also had a secret garden, trees with rope swings and no-go areas of tough kids. My range was also negotiated by fragments of woodland and privet-lined alleyways. I also used to walk down roads with my mother, the two of us imagining what life would be like if we lived in this or that house.

Socio-anthropologists say that humans tend to live in ostensibly tribal groupings. Whether you're in Swindon or the Amazon Basin you know roughly 500 people. Perhaps the same law applies to these childhood ranges – all things being equal kids will end up traversing the same distances in the same ways.

But they aren't equal – those things. One of the most traumatic moments of my own childhood was the day they painted a dotted white line down the middle of our road. My children won't be able to range as freely as my wife and I did until they're 12 or 13, and by then their sense of topography will be hopelessly distorted by seeing it in jump-cuts through the windows of cars.

We would all do well to remember this.

'I've tried living in a shack, but my lean-to is far nicer ...'

ACCELERATING TO A HALT

Some old cars are not so much examples of earlier vehicular forms – I dare say they still speak of 'carriage work' at Mitsubishi – as of houses. As a child I vividly remember riding in my godfather Bartle Frere's antique Rolls Royce Silver Ghost. He picked my father and I up from Peterborough station and we drove back to where he lived in Stamford, a fine bit of preservation in its own right.

In the back of the antique limo I marvelled at the First World War field dressings I found in the glove compartments; and goggled at the flower vases mounted by the windows. As the windows were sash-like (divided into upper and lower panels), they wouldn't have looked out of place in the façade of a townhouse. The car was rigidly segregated along class lines – communication between sealed rear and front compartments was via speaking trumpet, which again gave it the feeling more of an Edwardian dwelling with leaded windows than anything requiring unleaded.

Actually, I think my godfather liked converting transport into domestic architecture, rather than vintage cars, for he'd also made a cunning little shelf in his nonagenarian mother's prosthetic leg, so that she could handily truck her cigars about.

But Bartle, though eccentric, was by no means the only person driving around in the 1960s in a mobile hutment.

Do you remember Morris Travellers? I say remember, but there's still a fair number of them about the place. Morris Travellers! The foremost of the great half-timbered, Tudor-revival automobiles. What an absolutely bizarre and hilarious notion, driving around in something that should really be emphatically stationary and bordered by a carefully clipped privet hedge.

Imagine what it might be like to live in a mock-Tudor house and drive a Morris Traveller – you'd be hard put to know whether you were coming or going nowhere. It would be like the gag told by the American comedian Steven Wright: 'I've got an ansaphone on my car phone. The outgoing message says: "I'm sorry, I can't take your call right now, I'm in."'

I've always retained a sense of the car as a hut-on-wheels. Perhaps it's the nature of the life I've led – often mindlessly peripatetic – but all too often I've found myself in some lay-by near Droitwich, canted sideways in the driver's seat, eating a pork pie, a Cup-a-Soup being gently warmed by an element plugged into the fag lighter, while listening to *Woman's Hour*. At these moments, as in the eternities of childhood drives, the car has ceased to be a meaningful means of transport and is instead a form of housing. Nothing more, nothing less.

Of course, the Pina Farinas of this world are Vorticists to a man; and the whole tendency of serious car design this century has been towards greater fluidity and increased aerodynamics of form, both externally and internally. Now even bog-standard fleet cars like Vauxhall Cavaliers and Ford Mondeos come with astonishingly jazzy, allegedly ergonomic interiors. I hate these collections of hideous, etiolated kidney shapes. The sense of speed implied by these designs, is the terminal velocity of an excised organ slithering down a gutter.

There's no way – these designs squeak – that you can consider us anything but cars. Gone are the days when dirigibles had salons depending from them; gone are the days when flying boats had *en suite* bedrooms. But what I say is – what a ridiculous irony it is that as these vehicles have become more and more fitted to their full-frontal impulsion, so the opportunities have been radically curtailed. Let me put it another way. If I had to sit, grinding forward a few metres at a time, in heavy traffic for anything up to hours out of every day, I know which kind of car I'd prefer to do it in – Bartle's every time.

CUL-DE-SAC

I can still remember the particular colouring, texture and distribution of moss in the cracks of the paving stones outside my childhood home. I can remember the precise form of the wooden sconces that blocked the air vents inside my childhood home. I can remember the exact number of – five-year-old – paces it took to circumnavigate the garden of my childhood home. Of my parents I remember nothing.

All right, it's an exaggeration, but if you'd known my parents, not so much larger than life as completely devoid of context, you'd understand why editing them out has proved so irresistible. But I don't think that I'm being pathological or solipsistic, because the same is probably true of you. You in particular – being people who are professionally preoccupied by the built environment – probably have better visio-spatial recall than you do language (under which heading I would subsume almost all purely factual memory).

Hell, if I can remember air-vent details, you can probably run to types of MDF, or lengths of screws, as part of the ordinary substratum of recall. But the serious point is that the child's memories are the very rubric of the adult. If, as I did, you spent the entirety of your childhood in the same house, it can exert a lasting influence on you in diverse and subtle ways.

For me the three-bedroom, semi-detached house, with

privet-lined front and back gardens, useless faux shutters; red-brick built, featuring a garage of the same on the detached side (all of a couple of metres), and neighbours called Lewis and Mary Wein, constitutes the *locus classicus*. This is the primal house, the Ur-house, the very Platonic form of the word 'house'. It seems screamingly obvious to me.

But if I grew up in an Ur-house, the harsh fact of the matter is that I also grew up in an Ur-suburb. So primary was our suburb that it was even called *The* Hampstead Garden Suburb. Given that my father was an academic who specialised in the theory of urban planning, I had a very real sense, as a child, of actually coming to full, reflective, self-consciousness within a psychic synoecism.

Laid out on a series of long avenues which radiate from the chilling non-euphemism 'Central Square', the environs of the Suburb are a reification of the social ideals of its builders. Central Square itself is dominated by two churches – C of E and non-denominational – and Dame Henrietta Barnett's Girls School. Barnett was one of the guiding spirits of the 'burb. It was she who countenanced the provision of different sectors and types of housing within the 'burb, so as to embody, in privet, the social castes of the time. (Though there was no real provision for working-class families, merely 'artisans' cottages.)

Our semi was on Brim Hill, across the North Circular from the bulk of the 'burb, and very much at the non-U end of things. I was poised between the devil and the deep blue sea, because at around 12, when I was forced to abandon my RP in favour of Mockney, I had to say that I lived in East Finchley, the very acme of dull outer-London suburbs.

Anyway, by then the damage was done. I'd already spent

a lifetime staring across the valley at the rich folks on the hill. Or rather the square folks: because if there was one abiding impression that the 'burb left on me, it's that this quite substantial chunk of metropolis was entirely without any commercial premises. These were exiled to the periphery. Most notably – Barnett having been a temperance wowser herself – there were no pubs.

To grow up in an area with no pubs! It makes me want to weep. And to have grown up in an idealised, Kate Greenaway-inspired vision of the built environment? It makes me want to live the rest of my life with my arms buried to the elbow in the rotting entrails of the real thing.

MANDELSON: THE KENSINGTON YEARS

My week – architecture wise – has been entirely mediated by reading Donald Macintyre's excellent biography of Peter Mandelson; which is entitled – with delicious simplicity – *Mandelson* (HarperCollins, ludicrously seductive price point: £19.99). Now, Mandy's downfall, as we all know, was a function of appalling hubris, a mortgaging of his own sense of arrogant entitlement.* But before he got to that gaff on Northumberland Place in Notting Hill, you have to consider what property nightmares he'd sustained along the way.

To begin with there was his upbringing he shared, with me, in The Hampstead Garden Suburb. But whereas the Selfs were confined to the poor end of Lutyens's herbaceous vision, the Mandelsons were on Bigwood Road, up near Central Square. Now, is it any wonder that the suburb engendered in the young Peter an unrealistic view of what to expect from the rest of the country? Given that it is set out like an idealised, sub-bucolic polis, complete with socially-graduated housing, no pubs and ample green spaces upon which your canines may happily maculate.

* In December 1998, Peter Mandelson, then Minister without Portfolio in the Labour government, was forced to resign after revelations that he had bought his house with a loan from the Paymaster General, Geoffrey Robinson.

I'm not saying that The Hampstead Garden Suburb is slightly unreal – it's totally unreal. It stands in the same relation to a real suburb as Portmerion does to Palladio. I should know, I spent the first 16 years of my life there,and when it became time to go out into the wider world I was amazed to discover that there were parts of this sceptr'd isle where privet is a stranger and the diamond-patterned mullion has not been perpetuated. How much worse must it have been for Mandelson, whose first memories were of lording it on an eminence, gazing out over this leafy fiefdom?

How cruel it must have been for Mandelson to be exiled from his four-square, detached, natal home, and forced into a 'bijou' flat in Lambeth with 'a bed in the living room which folded back into the wall, and a tiny kitchen and bathroom.' Surely this experience alone (like Dickens's sojourn in the blacking factory) is sufficient to explain his burgeoning and idealistic desire for a large terraced property in one of London's most desirable areas? No, for Macintyre also informs us that for a while his subject had a flat in Farringdon, but that he never liked it because of the traffic noise. Indeed, he was prominent in a local residents' campaign against the rumbling.

But as if this weren't enough there was more humiliation to come. In 1984 Mandelson was compelled to buy a cottage near Ross-on-Wye in Hereford. Imagine it: locked out from the Cotswolds and driven to weekend in Ultima Thule; can there be any doubt that it was at this time Mandelson found himself considering whether or not a future Labour administration might approve considerable greenfield-site housing development?

In December 1989 Mandelson was selected as the

Labour Party candidate for Hartlepool and was dragooned into buying a four-bedroom house in Hutton Avenue. According to his biographer: 'The house ... has a large, homely, unmodernised kitchen; the study overlooks the front garden ... and the sitting room, comfortably but unremarkably furnished, is festooned with family photographs.' Macintyre goes on to state that: 'This is where the Labourist in Mandelson is still most at home.'

Indeed, for the Labourist in Mandelson is quite clearly a southern liberal poseur pretending to be a northern trade unionist, just like the rest of the New Labourists who run the country. No, none of us has ever wanted 'Oor Pete', as we've dubbed him, to feel at home there, we want him in his rightful element, swimming in the current of the *demimonde* which courses through west London. I was sorry to hear that in the wake of his resignation from the cabinet, Mandelson has decided to sell the property for a mere 20 per cent profit on his (and Gerry's) £500k investment. C'mon Peter, don't let the bastards grind you down! Don't let them force you out of your natural habitat. You owe it to those of us who voted Labour into office (and implicitly endorsed your ambitions) to keep on up that greasy property pole until you reach the very top. I like to think that Macintyre will be able to get tapping those keys again before too long, working on the next volume of your biography: *Mandelson: The Kensington Years*.

MANDELSON OF THE NORTH

SHOPPING IN SPACE

In 1976 the Brent Cross shopping centre was opened on the North Circular Road in north London. It was a revelation – the first indoor 'regional' shopping mall we'd ever seen in Britain. I remember that kids from my school used to go there just to hang out and admire the water feature in front of Fenwicks. I found Brent Cross a queasy sort of space to visit, its atriums and walkways redolent of fake open-airness. Ever since then I've been more or less incapable of eating at a food court in a shopping centre, for fear that an electronic bird will swoop over my table and crap on my fettucini.

In many parts of the world the enclosed shopping mall can be justified as a necessity of the climate – certainly this is true in the US. But in our temperate zone the mega-malls are being built on the fringes of our conurbations because of pressures upon the built environment. The first and foremost of these is, of course, the car. The weekly shop is almost unimaginable without the motorised boot-on-wheels – I know, I'm the one who does it in my home. As the cart track is to the market, so the six-lane urban beltway is to the shopping mall.

But the second and more insidious pressure, is our unwillingness to view shopping as an aspect of social and communal living. One of the sickest aspects of the abduction and killing of Jamie Bulger, was that his abductors were not stopped by any human, but 'seen' by a security camera in a shopping mall. I'm not so naïve as to imagine that this isn't the sort of thing that could have happened in an 'old fashioned' shopping environment, but the traditional street market, with its tightly demarcated zones of interraction – and hence observation – does seem to provide for a more personalised kind of purchasing.

Certainly people seem to feel this way. All over the country people go to street markets where they buy produce that is often more expensive than that they could buy in out of town shopping malls. The whole street-market phenomenon fades at one end into the tourist trade – like London's Portobello Road – and at the other into the car-boot sale, where people go to shop for a recreation.

Shopping enables parents to teach their children all manner of important things, from the correct way to comport themselves in public, to handling financial transactions, to making effective cost-benefit choices. But the large-scale, outer-urban shopping mall, with its mass anonymity and inflexible commercialism, is not by any means the ideal university.

THE WEINS WILL HEAR YOU

As I've had cause to remark, I grew up in that Platonic ideal of a 'hood, The Hampstead Garden Suburb in north London. Begun in 1907, at the instigation of the philanthropist Mrs (later Dame) Henrietta Barnett, the Suburb was intended to be a social test tube, within which the classes could safely react with one another. The plans were drawn up by Raymond Unwin and Barry Parker, who designed Letchworth Garden City in 1903. Lutyens was responsible for some of the better buildings, including the brick-heavy churches (Free and Anglican) which dominate the prosaically named Central Square. But while good, vernacular building was done in the core of the suburb, the fringes – where we lived – were full of less impressive, post-First World War semis.

We lived next to Mrs Ruben, who was a widow. I never knew anything about her save for that. Incredible. Her gardens, front and back, were immaculate, almost sterile. The kind of gardens that need dusting rather than weeding. I have only distant memories of the interior of her house. I must have gone in a couple of times as a very small child. All that remains are impressions of curved banquettes, glass-topped furniture, billowing nets, and the onslaught of furniture polish. It's not much considering the first 16 years of my life abutted 16 of the last years of hers.

It's not much considering that during this span we mic-turated, masticated, mused and, in my case, ejaculated, within inches of one another.

But then the semi has always been an odd hybrid, com-bining the close proximity living of the lower-class terrace, with the splendid isolation of the posh bucolic villa. The first semis to appear in the world were on the Eyre estate, St John's Wood, in the 1790s. It seems apt that semis should have been anonymously authored because these dwellings can reinforce alienation, just as much as they encourage neighbourliness.

We knew the Weins, who lived on the other side (and whose property was divided from ours by a garage, three feet of privet, and two paths), a bit better. Lewis and Mary Wein owned a dry-goods wholesale business in Ken-tish Town called 'LewMar'. They were a fussy, Jewish couple of indeterminate age who had an adopted daugh-ter. You could tell she was adopted because she looked nothing at all like the Weins. She was twice as big as them for a start. Their household was Rubenesque when com-pared to our own, with nets, glass tops, furniture polish and all. But in one respect we were highly compatible: both families were resolutely dysfunctional and subject to loud rowing. The climax of the bellowing *chez* Self was normally accompanied by my mother's hissed imprecation to 'Be quiet, the Weins will hear us!' To this day, I cannot raise my voice without the profound anxiety that I am being eavesdropped on by a middle-aged Jewish dry-goods wholesaler.

'The front elevation asserts its individuality by pic-turesque variations in details, though the house is in fact exactly the same in height and plan as all its neighbours.'

So wrote Michael Robbins of the semi. This was true of the houses on our road, except for the 'picturesque variations in details', for there were none. Or rather, just the one. Each the houses had sets of faux, slatted shutters on either side of the top windows. They didn't make the houses look as if they were in Provence (which is presumably what was intended), but they did provide an opportunity for the householder to paint them a different colour to those of the adjoining properties. Ours were blue, the Weins' were green, Mrs Ruben's were black.

I took my children back there the other day to see where I grew up. I hated suburbia and got out as quickly as I could, but driving out there from the inner city, what struck me first is what strikes everybody else: the space, the lack of on-road parking, the greenery … I feel an acute reversion to type coming over me.

ACTON UPSIDE DOWN

During my – comparatively speaking – wilder years, I had
the good fortune to spend six months on a working visa in
Australia. My father emigrated there in the early 1980s
determined to extend his career beyond that of his close
contemporary, Enver Hoxha. He took up a senior research
fellowship at the Australian National University in Canberra. Canberra is, depending on which way you view it,
either an inspired piece of garden city development, or an
ancient Aboriginal word meaning 'Milton Keynes'.

My father had been chairman of the Town and Country
Planning Association and an enthusiastic disciple of Frederick Osborne. My Dad referred reverentially to him as
'FJO'. We once visited him at his home, which wasn't far
from our own, in a nearby part of The Hampstead Garden
Suburb. Even as a child I think I was aware of the Russian
doll implications of this elderly planner inside a semi-
detached house, inside a planned suburb.

When I first visited my father in Canberra in the early
1980s, he was living just off the campus in a charmless
cul-de-sac called … wait for it … Brian Lewis Crescent.
Not only was there that astonishing piece of nomencla-
ture, but said crescent was located in the suburb of …
Acton. It had been blazing sunshine in Sydney, where I'd
sat in a solidly good restaurant, looking out over the
shimmering bitumen, eating a big steak, drinking a vast,

tannin-heavy red wine. Then I took the short-haul 200 miles over the Great Divide and descended into a drizzly immensity of hedges, verges, shopping malls and dual carriageways.

In the first shock of being in Acton in the rain, I found myself in the half-light of the following dawn, jogging along the shores of the artificial lake which forms the jewel, as it were, in the crown of the capital garden city. Astonishing concept, the sovereign water feature.

It was then that I began to realise the incontrovertible truth about life, that no matter how far you may travel in this world, you will still occupy the same volume of space.

My father's take on Canberra is, perforce, entirely different. He likes to stand on one of the precincts of Central Circuit, the somnolent hub of this drowsy conurbation, sweep one of his bolster arms so as to encompass a brace of the radial avenues, and proclaim: 'Amazing, isn't it? You wouldn't believe for a second that you're standing in the very core of a city of a quarter/third/half of a million.' (He's been saying this now for nigh on 20 years.)

It's true enough – not only wouldn't you believe it; you quite possibly couldn't believe it, such is the reposeful face of this lovely capital. Anyway, there's little point in knocking Canberra. Worse than that, over the years I've come, with grinding, high-torque predictability, to agree with his view of the place. Not only does it not feel like you're in a city when you're in the city, you can also get all the way out of the city without feeling that you're travelling through one.

THE ORIGIN OF THE SPECIES

In Darwin there are two basic architectural approaches to dealing with the monsoon climate. But before I get into that I had better explain to you where and what Darwin is. Its inhabitants labour under the profound delusion that their berg, if not exactly at the epicentre of global consciousness, is at any rate well known. This is because it's the only town in the Northern Territory of Australia of any size whatsoever. To the east and to the west there are many thousands of kilometres before you enter anything even resembling a built-up area; and to the north there's the Arafura sea, followed by Timor, the westernmost extremity of the unravelling Indonesian archipelago.

Thus Darwin, with its 60,000-odd inhabitants, sees fit to style itself, at one and the same time, the 'closest white city to the equator'; and 'Australia's most multicultural city'. When I lived there in the early 1980s the urban fabric still bore the marks and scars of the hurricane which had torn through ten years previously. This had lain waste to the hippy encampments on the beach and gouged great grooves through the very centre of town.

Unfortunately the economy of Darwin is dominated by subsidies from the Australian Federal Government; the Northern Territory – as its name implies – does not have statehood, but is rather a Federal satrap, within which the problems of the aboriginals can be tidied away, or 'dealt with'. In 1983–4 I was responsible – laughable though it may seem – for undertaking a study of the demand for building land in the Territory. Not a problem, you might have thought, in an area six times the size of the British Isles. Needless to say, none of the traditional methods an economist would employ for such a forecast (demographic projections; rate of household formation; land values etc.) were applicable in Darwin's case. Rather, the sole variant effecting the demand for building land was the rate of the Federal subsidy itself.

Sixteen years later, while the population itself has not significantly increased, the entrenched Federal bureaucracy has seen to it that there's been massive suburban infill. Darwin and its environs now stretch over an area of hundreds of square kilometres. The suburban jungles are interconnected by broad clearways; and where there be park, there be many many pieces of park furniture. It reminded me of nothing so much as one of those computer simulation games, like Sim City or in this case, Sim Park, where the touch of a button can summon up in a flash another pixelated chunk of property and infrastructure.

The most inappropriate and tasteless addition to Darwin's built environment is something called Cullen Bay. This is a marina development around a concreted dock, which features a horrific synthesis between South Fork and a shopping mall. I would swear to you that I've never seen a more gauche collection of sub-Californian *nouveau-riche* dwellings, were it not for the fact that nowadays I see them everywhere I go. But there is a delicious irony at work here, for the one thing the Cullen Bay buildings don't appear to be is typhoon-proof.

The two architectural ways of coping with the monsoon

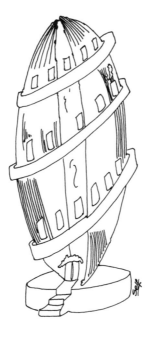

Bivalve apartments: tenants come and go, the developer extracts their nutrients.

are either to build a traditional, stilt house, with walls made permeable (by Venetian slats, raffia etc.), in the hope that the winds will blow straight through; or to have a storm room, a core box of concrete capable of withstanding the worst a tsunami has on offer. Many residents adopt both approaches, having stilt houses with storm rooms beneath. But Cullen Bay is just the usual chowder of crap condos, dragged up and the paint slapped on. While I was in Darwin the big news was that the marina had been invaded by an aggressive pest called the black-striped mussel. So prevalent was this bivalve that the local paper featured a photograph of a chair which had been submerged in the waters of the marina for five minutes, then withdrawn entirely encrusted with the bumptious bivalves.

Eco-warriors of my acquaintance muttered that this was only to be expected, given that the development was slap-bang on top of one of the most important aboriginal sacred sites in the locality. There's that, and there's also the inevitable environmental consequences of attempting to whack concrete atop mangrove swamp. At the moment the best chances for the tasteless flatlets (which are on offer for a free six-month trial should any readers wish to relocate) are that the black-striped mussels get to them before the next big wind, forming a storm-proof encrustation.

LYING IS TRYING

I'm trying, believe me, I'm trying. Though, that being said, I once had a supremely annoying therapist who used to say to me: 'Trying is lying', then increased my irritation by continuing, 'go on, try and get up from that chair. See – trying is lying.' But I'm not lying, I phoned the company who handle press relations and spoke to a Mr Barlow at Barratt Homes, who, when I enquired about visiting a Barratt home for the millennium, immediately sussed me: 'I suppose you'll be taking the piss out of it, won't you?' I demurred; he said he'd see what he could do.

I imagined him going to meet with the secret committee of Barratt, an intense convocation of middle-aged, shirt-sleeved men, sitting round a white plastic table, underneath a Perspex carport. I await Mr Barlow's intercession with these powers-that-build; and in the meantime I want to float some architectural observations on the Monica Lewinsky affair.

Virginia sandstone has a lot to answer for. If there's one thing of which you cannot accuse the Founding Fathers of America, it's a want of grandiosity. Contemporary Washington, with its teasing layout – doughnut of gross poverty surrounding the jam of imposing neoclassical architecture – has to be the most perfect synecdoche of the state the world's in. Be that as it may, its founders built it with the specific aim of intimidating foreign visitors who, presumably, were intended to find themselves labouring, ant-like, across the acres of sward beneath Capitol Hill, quaking in their ill-fitting European boots.

The White House, which has the same painted Virginia sandstone façade as the Capitol, is a less testosterone-fuelled, mock-Palladian gaff. Such is the want of tradition in the US that it's difficult for us to appreciate quite how much spiritual fervour is invested by the people in this building. The Capitol – and by extension the White House – has been replicated in state capital after capital through the hinterland; and when you hear stateside commentators bemoaning the way that the President has 'demeaned his office', they are speaking very literally.

The irony is that the Oval Office complex, within which these desecrations occurred, is a relatively dinky collection of rooms, no bigger overall than an average provincial English solicitor's offices. Indeed, there's barely room in the Oval Office itself to swing a cat, let alone a *jolie laide*, like Ms Lewinsky. Indeed, it's fair to say that it would have been bizarre if a satyromaniac like Clinton hadn't managed to penetrate her, simply by walking into the place. And by the same token, isn't it hard not to feel that her obsession was not a little nurtured by the very cosiness of this oval hub of power?

The whole episode puts me in mind of Kafka's lines: 'Leopards enter the temple and desecrate the sacred vessels. This occurs so frequently that it becomes incorporated into the ritual.' Kafka knew a fair bit about the awkward elisions when architectural and power structures collide; indeed he wrote a whole novel about the US, *Amerika,* without ever visiting the place, which described the cities and buildings in minute detail.

Kafka could do this creatively, but for most of us our ignorance of centres of power makes us prey to their architectural histrionics. But just think about it. What can be more absurd, in an alleged democracy, than institutional buildings designed to intimidate? Yet everywhere we look we see them. No wonder the London mob looked on appreciatively and bayed with delight when the Palace of Westminster burnt to the ground in 1834.

And who is the United Nations meant to impress? Who is meant to be intimidated by its grand assembly hall, with its amphitheatre of ranked bureaux, and its podium suitable for the Mekon? Is this aimed at us? I hardly think so, as the status of the UN is at a nadir all over the globe, and especially in the boonies of the US itself. Perhaps the whole UN plaza should be turned over to the IMF and painted black?

Or not. We may still need the UN to rail impotently at the alien invaders when they turn up – clearly it's aimed at them. Frankly, I'm fairly certain that they won't be in the least impressed by it. Indeed, they'd probably be far more likely to come in peace if we built a parliament building that reflected genuine, humane aspirations in a harmonious way.

Whether the same could be said for Clinton and his ilk is another matter.

The shock of the old.

tion of old street-front properties in inner urban areas became absolutely *de rigueur* for any middle-class families with style aspirations. They, in order to confirm their superiority, poured scorn upon people who moved into new houses that were externally fashioned in mock-period styles. Meanwhile, of course, they were moving into period houses and internally fashioning them so as to appear new. Such are the queer ironies of history.

Out in Watford, on the edge of Nascott Wood, an ancient, preserved piece of woodland, the small development of 17 Barratt homes was an innocent enough spectacle. Spread along either side of a cul-de-sac leading to the wood, they were sufficiently higgledy-piggledy – some ranged back from the road around an inner court, the rest with different heights, and staggered elevations – not to fill me with the Brookside horrors, the state of screaming claustrophobia I enter when a close becomes just too … close.

Bob and I sat and chatted in the living room of the show house, which was built – I hope I've got this right – according to the 'Salisbury' pattern. The 'Premier Collection' which is the Barratt pattern book, has 700 different kinds of house design in it, all the way from single-bedroom flats on up. Presumably these include the available ranges of fitted-kitchen and bathroom styles, which come inclusive; though I didn't establish whether there was an option on the carpeting as well.

This, Bob and I bridled over a little. 'What colour would you call it?' I asked. 'Mmm,' he replied thoughtfully, 'in the days when Habitat was a new concept I suppose I'd've called it oatmeal, but now … well …' I could see a profound struggle was being waged within him, '… I suppose you'd have to say it was …' his voice was barely more than a whisper, '... beige.'

Overall the house was pleasing and predictable enough. It would be easy enough to take the piss out of it – but that's not the point: no matter if it's Hyacinth Bucket's gaff, no home is ever a show home. Anyway, it was the externals that really interested me; for here they all were, the standard features of inter-war suburban façades: the barge boards and coins; the porches and the carved-stone lintels; the mock beams and bay windows – all back in place unto the next generation.

The strange thing was that none of it really looked that 'mock'; and in a sense, I suppose, it wasn't. These weren't mock-Tudor effects, they were mock-mock-Tudor. Can you really have a mock-mock style? Surely it's just a style in its own right?

It was with questions such as these buzzing in my brow, that I headed back towards my early nineteenth-century townhouse in the inner city. People are such snobs. Why shouldn't anyone live in a well appointed, mock-mock-Tudor home, entirely free from any sense of stylistic inferiority? Mind you, the Barratt homes that I really didn't like the look of were those inspired by the Quinlan Terryites of the 1980s. You know the kind of thing – mock-Regency I suppose you'd call it.

Christ confuses an estate agent: 'In my father's houses are many mansions …'

THREE QUOINS IN A FOUNTAIN

A lot of people say I'm a pedant; I've heard it muttered, round darkling corners, that I'm something of a sesquipedalian as well. I wouldn't deny that. The essential meaning of language is a function of its usage; so if our tongue is to live and writhe, all of its parts must continue to be employed.

Actually, questions of language and architecture are neither recondite nor irrelevant. Any profession constructs itself – its very sense of itself – around the deployment of its own arcana, expressed in its own technical vocabulary. As architects, civil engineers, quantity surveyors, whatever, the way you gear into the practical manipulation of the material world is as thoroughly mediated by language, as it is by any prong, blade, bolt, girder or scoop.

I was hired by Louise Rogers, editor of *Building Design* (whose name, for obvious, Freudian reasons, I am completely unable to recall in polite society), to write a column which would refract an image of the built environment back to the profession, slanted by my emphatically lay perspective. But how do I retain my lay purity? Do I abjure learning more about architecture and building as rigorously as I may? If people begin discussing architecture technically, while standing by me in a lift, do I hush them up?

This is all leading somewhere; the poisonous gleet gathers to a head! I'm not usually troubled by responses to

The return of the bumper sticker manufacturer.

my writing, but my column a couple of weeks ago on Barratt Homes garnered a massive response: two letters, one of them from Bob Barlow himself, the independent PR who showed me round the Barratt estate. Both my correspondents felt they had to point out my ludicrous misspelling – and hence, apparently, misapprehension – of the term 'quoin', in the following context: '... all the standard features of interwar suburban façades: the barge boards and coins; the porches and the carved stone lintels; the mock beams and bay windows ...'

But according to my *Shorter* OED: 'Quoin (koin) sb. (var. of coin.)' And I don't think anyone could state it more clearly than that! So, who's right about this, the professionals who actually employ the term, or the lexicographers who plot, as it were, a word's career? I suppose it has to be the latter; and anyway, architecture shouldn't be a profession grounded in the vernacular orthography of a term for a wall embellishment. Certainly not while there's such madness all around. Consider the Bull Ring on London's South Bank, for so many years the focal point for that parodying of the built environment, which are the homes of the homeless.

I had a delirious architectural experience a couple of years ago, when, having reeled out of the precincts of Somerset House – wherein my fiduciary *cojones* were being amputated by a divorce action – I staggered across Waterloo Bridge and descended into the Bull Ring. My reasoning was that having had all of my capital (which like that of most of the bourgeoisie was enshrined in bricks and mortar) taken from me, I belonged in the company of same.

I pitched up in the company of Howie and his pals, sitting outside a substantial bash (at least three separate cardboard-partitioned cubicles), and discussing the vicissitudes of life over a convivial litre of Night Train. Howie was heavy on the face metal; but despite his homelessness, his alcoholism, and having been ripped out from the fabric of society, he still had a vision of a better future. This vision was contained in the several thousand bottles he had collected from around the Bull Ring with a view to having them recycled. He showed them to me, file upon file of them, brown, green, white, and two whole wheelie bins of cans.

I wonder what's happened to Howie and his Pinteresque recycling mission now? Now that the concrete aorta of the Bull Ring has been stoppered with a plug of new construction? Who knows, but one nice irony is that the columnar block they're erecting here, slap bang in the middle of one of the city's busiest roundabouts, has been sheathed with glass.

And naturally, there isn't a coin – or a quoin for that matter – in sight.

MOCK-MOCK

Finally, Bob Barlow's intercession with the mysterious powers who control Barratt Homes paid off, and this morning I found myself wheeling north, to Watford, to experience the Barratt home for the millennium.

Bob had been a bit worried that I was only going to take the piss. He doesn't see anything funny about a firm, the second biggest house builder in the country, employing approximately 26,000 people in 22 divisions. He doesn't smile too wryly when his firm – responsible for innovative developments, all the way from Pierhead in London's Docklands to Penarth Marina, Cardiff and back again – is entirely subsumed to a hackneyed stereotype of shirt-sleeved, middle-aged men, sitting on white plastic furniture under Perspex carports. Oh no.

My wife pointed out to me before I left that when she was a child, growing up in industrial Lanarkshire, a Barratt home was the last word in sophistication and aspiration. When she was in the sixth form she managed to make friends with a girl who lived in a Barratt home, but after a while the relationship floundered over irreconcilable differences.

I suppose the real demonisation of the Barratt home by those whom Bob – excepting present company, my jaw was wired – termed 'the chattering classes', must have really got underway at the same time that the recolonisa-

'We were interested to see what it would be like if a window tax was
levied …'

VERNACULAR RIGHTS

In Fermanagh, Northern Ireland, my friend Carlo, together with his wife and burgeoning family, inhabit a converted nineteenth-century schoolhouse. They haven't gone to the lengths of putting in pin-prick lights and modular kitchens, but nor have they slavishly stayed within the parameters of the original building. The result is a curiously elegant dwelling, focused on the former schoolroom, filled with light from a bank of high windows.

But all is not so mellow in the local built environment. As we drive into Enniskillen, the local town, Carlo fulminates against the way it's been developed: 'This was a superb example of an old, garrison town, now they've ripped the heart out of it with modern development!' This is true enough, though I forbear from mentioning a fact that Carlo knows only too well: the IRA have had a good go at ripping the heart out of Enniskillen as well.

'It's the zoning I can't abide,' he continues. 'See, this is the limit of building allowed, so naturally the developers put up their new estates on the limit, and the rest of the land becomes so much ragged infill – it's ruining the character of the place.'

The character of the place is actually fairly strange, for all sorts of reasons. Enniskillen is set on the shores of Lough Erne, and styles itself 'the island town' – it's in fact on a narrow isthmus. You're insistently aware of the presence of large bodies of water – either lying on the earth or falling from the sky – as you move around the environs. The rumpled counterpane of the immediate countryside, with the backdrop of distant hills, give an odd sub-Alpine feel to the area. It was no surprise to me to learn from Carlo that the vast majority of tourists who hire luxury cruisers on the Lough are Germans or Swiss.

In the afternoon I take a walk from Carlo's house to a local landmark, Topped Mountain. On the way I pass a Presbyterian church. This is a veritable spear of Gothic revival planted in the green haunch of Ireland, so quiveringly sharp does the spire seem in the damp afternoon light. In the graveyard a lot of the headstones are disturbingly new; death's tiny estate of shiny granite.

Trudging on along the road I pass the premises-cum-dwelling of a local glass magnate. Both buildings represent the acme of modern Irish vernacular. Both buildings are bungaloid, all vast picture windows and steeply pitched roofs. Leading up to them are impressive, sweeping driveways. The gateposts are surmounted by concrete statues of eagles, bigger than life size. The effect is bizarre to say the least – like calling on the hall of the mountain king only to find that he's keenly interested in DIY.

Later Carlo and I perambulate in a different direction and he fulminates against the way the new vernacular has displaced the old: 'Look!' he says, gesturing at a substantial, two-storey farmhouse about 400 metres back from the lane. 'Look at the way they've ripped out all the old windows and put in the flaps and pictures; and they've replaced the slates with ones that won't weather; and then they'll dash it in some way –' '– But actually Carlo,' I broke in, 'this particular house isn't that bad, is it?' He took a closer look. 'Well, yes, I suppose you're right.' And this conversion *was* interesting. The way in which the size of the windows had been increased, combined with the new rendering, created a strange hybrid, but not at all unattractive.

We strolled on. 'Now that's interesting,' Carlo pointed at a yellow, corrugated-iron house some way down the hill, 'that's a style of building in tin that returning emigrants brought back with them from Australia, tin roof, then tin walls stuffed with whatever for insulation.' I regarded the tin house, which with its strutted verandah out front wouldn't have looked out of place in some Northern Queensland settlement.

We walked on in silence. I don't know what Carlo was thinking, but I was considering that the people have a right to their vernacular architecture, wherever it comes from and whatever it looks like. After all, the picture windows of Fermanagh are designed to be looked out of, not into.

BAD TIMING

Even writing for a specialist journal such as *Building Design* it's unwise to monkey around too much with the future. Cassandra would still be a force for ill, even if she merely published her dolorous predictions in the pages of *Licensed Victualling Today*.

At any rate, following last week's 'humorous' outing in the guise of a NATO commander with a view to attacking the command and control centres of Middle England (see page 15), this week's is, predictably, an account of nearly being bombed.

Not that the evening started off that way. I set out from our house in Vauxhall at around 17.30 with a view to meeting my wife, Deborah, at a preview theatre on D'Arblay Street in Soho. She was charged with the odious task of writing something for her rag about the new film *Notting Hill*, a tale of property prices, the minor public-school educated and 'village' London.

Now, as I've had cause to say before: I don't live in a village – I live in a city! Got that? A city. It's big – indeed, it's vast; and it's been vast for nigh on 1000 years. In order to emphasise to myself just how big it is, and just how much I live in it, I like to walk into central London. Try it yourselves, all you scryers of the concreted firmament; if you want to really apprehend what it is you're doing with the built environment, don't just go for a modest site visit, get out and walk a good three or four miles through built-up areas, *then* you'll understand what it's all about.

Anyway, hortatory moment over. Since I reach the Embankment some ten minutes after I leave the house, and thereafter, until I attain Horse Guards I am continually in sight of Big Ben, I am always acutely aware of time on these walks. So, at 17.50 I was in Parliament Square; at 18.05 I was ascending the steps by the ICA and marvelling once again at the size of the Duke of York's column; at 18.10 I was in Piccadilly (still no sign of the much-vaunted, new, fully computerised Coca-Cola hoarding); and at around a 18.15 I was strolling up Wardour Street, passing the mouth of Old Compton Street.

At 18.20 I liaised with Deborah in D'Arblay Street, and around 12 minutes later we were watching Hugh Grant deploy the pseudo-upper class characteristics which are adjudged seductive by the film-going public. (Though in all honesty how anyone can suspend disbelief in Grant as a seducer any more is beyond me, when we all know that if he doesn't succeed in getting a girl for free, he'll simply go out and pay for one.) We were approximately 300 metres away from the explosion that blew out the interior of the Admiral Duncan pub at around 18.40. Three hundred metres – and a world apart. We heard nothing, central London preview theatres being well insulated. And knew nothing until we emerged from the make-believe 'village' of Richard Curtis's imagination, into the very real and very traumatised city which the rest of us inhabit.

Look, I know that Curtis was writing a romantic comedy (I also know Curtis himself, and he's a universally liked, Jill Dando of a man), so rules of verisimilitude don't apply, but I can't help hating the way in which *Notting*

Hill transmogrifies a big, vital, architecturally exciting, cosmopolitan city, into a ditsy, biscuit-tin lid, all-white enclave. One of most ridiculous discontinuities in this tissue of imaginings, was the idea that William Thacker, the Grant character, who runs a book shop on Portobello Road, and owns an adjacent property, is a failure. A failure! The man's sitting on around £1.5 million worth of real estate! If only all of life's failures could be so sweet.

As we came out from the film we saw on a television in the foyer the news that there had been a bombing in central London. As we walked out into the street I could hear the unaccustomed silence of an evacuated Soho. The person who bombed the Admiral Duncan may have wanted to believe that he was bombing London's 'gay village' – but for those of us who really live here and now, he was bombing us all.

'This village isn't big enough for the two of us!'

EAST OF EDEN

The great founding father of structural anthropology, Claude Levi-Strauss, hypothesised that all of the world's great cities were constructed on an east-to-west axis that reflected a hard socio-economic gradient: the wealthy to the west; the poor to the east.

Levi-Strauss saw this as evidence of a collective and instinctual tendency on the part of human societies, inter-reacting with the built environment. Other theorists of the urban scape have offered more prosaic explanations: that the prevailing trade winds – certainly in the northern hemisphere – mean that the shit always hits the fan to the east.

Whatever the causal explanation, the observed phenomenon certainly always used to hold true for the Great Wen. And, of course, EastEnders endureth. I think that this analysis of the city's human geography is far more convincing than the estate agency twaddle about 'village London'; a bogus jargon which has inspired the creation of numerous pseudo-communities. (My personal favourite is 'Methrovia'; a tiny grid of gentrification centred around Methwyn Road in Kennington, south London.)

I make some apology for writing about London again, but I feel certain that our friends in the north are in absolutely no doubt that we are their enemies in the south, and this goes a long way towards justifying what follows.

As early as the sixteenth century there were grave concerns that London's viral spread would be fatal for the nation. James I quipped, 'Soon London will be all England.' It was certainly true that population was leeched from the hinterland – and this continues to this day. But from the early twentieth century, when Bazalgette's main sewers were in place, and Yerkes' vision of the Underground had already inspired more stops and connections than we have had until this era, it was infill all the way.

The population pullulated first into Metroland, then into Roseland. Sir Frederick Osborne's vision of a protective 'green belt' around the metropolis, girdled by the so-called 'garden cities' came into being. From Enfield to Swanley was all dusty infill, and it disrupted the natural structure of the urban environment as drastically as the car. Indeed, its final, awful confirmation has been provided by the car; *pace* the AA's appeal during severe jams on the M25, that drivers shouldn't attempt to find their way via alternative routes, for fear of gridlocking the entire south east of England.

So, planners and listings magazines spout bullshit about 'villages', while the prime minister witters on about 'community'. What change from Major I ask myself? One fact about the built environment in London is inescapable: the very populace are ignorant of its true physical characteristics. How many people have actually stood at the mouth of the Thames? Not many of the middle class for sure – they tend to debouch to the west, heading for Gloucestershire, Wiltshire and other twee destinations. But the old EastEnders go east to Sheppey, Grain and Southend, where they dabble their feet in effluent and Weil's disease.

Levi-Strauss would have approved.

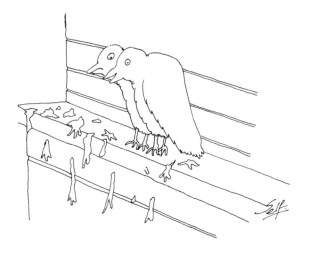

'God! This place is a toilet …'

SMOOTH CHEEK – ROTTEN JOWL

My five-year-old daughter has been pestering me for the past couple of months to go on one of the open-topped, double-decker buses that ply their way around the tourist sights of central London. Understandably I have resisted these pressures. Why on earth would you want to perambulate, at ridiculously slow speeds, around streets and buildings that you encounter in a grinding, frustrating, workaday fashion for the entire time? The answer is that the experience is enlightening.

We boarded the bus on the south side of Lambeth Bridge and proceeded east. The first thing I noticed was how much the tour directs your gaze upwards. Professional architects and people employed in the building industry may be well used to surveying the city in this fashion, but for most of us the pressures of urban living literally bow us down, so that we seldom direct our vision above the second storey.

London, looked up to on a cold, bright, winter morning became an altogether lighter, airier and more pleasing place. Another factor was simply encountering the centre of the city in a non-working, non-hurrying context (it was a Sunday morning). Anyone charged with trying to make the city a more 'friendly' environment would do well to remember this: get the people who actually live here to play here as well.

My new perspective afforded me a much better grasp on the material condition of the built environment. Without the bus trip, I would never have noticed the enormous chunk of concrete cladding that has simply dropped off the ghastly – and now empty – hexagonal, brutalist office block which constitutes the roundabout on the south side of Westminster Bridge. I also began to pick out the numbers of other empty and derelict properties there were along our route. Seeing a large abandoned premises hard by Waterloo Station, I was struck by the extent to which we render the built environment curiously undifferentiated by our desire to see our cities as 'rational' constructions.

Nothing could be further from the truth. In London the smooth cheek is always hard against the rotten jowl. As our bus bumbled along, over Waterloo Bridge and into the City of London, I was more and more impressed by this fantastic, raddled, 2000-year-old palimpsest of construction upon demolition upon construction.

I wish I could have said the same for my five-year-old – but then her feet were very cold.

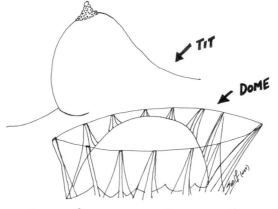

TIT

DOME

Suggestions for What Might Go in The Millennium Dome
NO: 1 ≈ An Enormous Tit   (like P. Mandelson)

DOWNRIVER

It's a commonplace observation that London is a city which turns its back on its river. Indeed, such is the capacity of the city to turn its back that there's even a building – the Queen Elizabeth Hall on the South Bank – which has itself performed a peculiar volte-face. Of course, the modern city has good reason for disdaining the Thames. For a start the river is inconveniently curved in its course. If only it were a nice horizontal line, confirming with physical geography the hemispheric impression that Londoners like to have of their city. Oh for a London in which Westminster wasn't south of Waterloo!

The second problem is that London's river has proved itself to be unsuitable for modern cargo ships. Gone are the days when you could stand at the top of the Pool of London and see thousands of vessels docking and unloading to the east. Gone are the days when London was not only the workshop of the world, but also the entrepôt of Europe. Since the early 1960s when the Docks began closing, the Thames has become more and more of a backwater. There have been many attempts to capitalise on the river as a possible transport route, in particular a flurry when the new offices began going up on the Isle of Dogs during the 1980s. But despite the appalling congestion on London roads no one, as yet, has been able to make a passenger ferry service on the Thames profitable.

This may be about to change. I note that there's a new ferry coming on stream for the millennium, in order – you guessed it – to ferry passengers to that marvellous structure known only as 'Rogers's Tit'. Despite the fact that the boats allocated for this run have ads for Coca-Cola on them, I do hope that it proves a success. For, in the meantime, if you want to travel on the river and you don't have your own vessel, you're obliged to embark on one of the tourist boats which depart for Greenwich from the Westminster Pier.

I did this trip twice during half-term week; a function, I suppose, of having far too many children. (As Groucho famously remarked: 'I like my cigar – but I know when to take it out.') I was alive to the possibility of Marchioness-style incidents, but although the boats are still rackety and run down there was nothing unduly worrying about the voyage. Nothing, that is, save for the commentary given by one of the crew members.

Now, all you out in architecture land; all of you who are proud of, and care about, our built environment, there is one constituency in our capital which it is vital you address. There is one extremely influential portion of the populace, whose good favour you should earnestly enjoin. I refer, of course, to said crew. On both of our trips downriver we were treated to a commentary on the buildings on either bank, a commentary that for many of the millions of tourists who visit our city will be the only comprehensive information they receive on London's built environment.

And what was that message? Old buildings = good. New buildings = bad. Our crewman had nothing but snide cracks to make about the following: the Queen Elizabeth Hall, the National Theatre, Bankside, Butler's Wharf,

Canary Wharf. Indeed, such was his contempt for all of the new buildings between Bankside and the Isle of Dogs that he couldn't even be bothered to keep up the commentary. I could see his point of view. When he told us that he'd begun his working life on the river on the site of Hay's Galleria, when it was still a functioning dock, I realised that his bitterness was a result of having spent his entire career watching an industry decline. Still, while I myself have considerable doubts about the merits of a lot of London's newer buildings, I don't like the idea of our visitors being subjected to this stream of bile.

The crew make great play during their commentary about how they're unpaid. They then pass the hat and get generous contributions. Perhaps someone who cares a little bit more about the city as it is now should be encouraged to give these commentaries? After all, there's only so much glorious past anybody can stick – what about a glorious future?

SPIRIT OF THE BEEHIVE

When one million people congregate to watch the corpse of a 36-year-old woman being dragged around the centre of town on a cart, you have to ask yourself what's going on. This is an entirely reasonable response to crowd behaviour of any form. As Konrad Lorenz so succinctly puts it: 'When I see the mass of people running in one direction, my natural inclination is to head the opposite way.' But for those of us who are concerned with the built environment the symbolism of the Princess of Wales' death and interment is inescapable – and intriguing. Naturally the high-speed auto death – 122 miles per hour into a series of concrete piles that would make Le Corbusier himself smile with brutalist fervour – is freighted with its own antinomies of hard/soft, public/private, SIPS/espaliered; but more curious is the cart drag.

Starting off in front of Buck House – held by the national psyche to be a kind of Platonic ideal of the English stately home, but as graphically undistinguished as Babar's Celesteville – the *Reservoir Dogs* line-up of princes (plus Earl Spencer) went to work. Literally. They strode down the Mall towards Trafalgar Square and beyond it – the City. This chord – between money and the Crown – is the real song of power in the land, and always has been. Having paid their homage in this direction, the cortege wheeled right before Admiralty Arch and headed down

Horse Guards' Parade. This – insofar as the cart drag represented a symbolic revisiting of conventional authority sites – was entirely correct. Nelson was a commoner, and Trafalgar Square has as much of a whiff of Peterloo as Waterloo about it – *vide* the Poll Tax riots. But at the head of Horse Guards' are the Cabinet War Rooms – top military site – and then it's plain sailing into Parliament Square, and the Abbey. Here the executive and the established church face off against one another, and effect yet another disjunction of the poor woman.

In Stanislav Lem's novel *Solaris*, scientists studying an enormous ocean on a distant planet realise that it's actually an entity, when it begins to produce numerous vast architectonic structures. The scientists find, upon analysing these 'symetriads', that their shapes are physical analogues of complex mathematical equations.

Lem is making a point here about the urban environment, and the lesson is that when you furnish the centre of a capital city, you are providing a four-dimensional, scale model of the obtaining hierarchy. If the cart drag teaches us anything it's that she really was a queen bee, and our behaviour has largely been anti-autonomous, pro-authoritarian, and bad for the built environment.

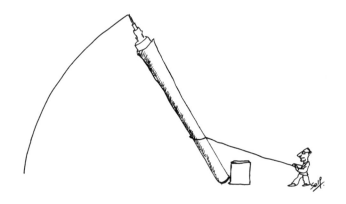

Drawing to scale.

BIG KNOB

News has reached me of a Saudi prince's intention to build the highest skyscraper in Arabia. Because of zoning laws in Riyadh, the top 900 feet or so of this mammoth glass and steel knob, will be empty space, a steel latticework forming the eye of a tremendous needle, large enough – the prince says – for a Boeing 737 to fly through. Avoiding the obvious gags about rich men, the prince's vaunting ambition struck me afresh as I mused on the very real extent to which the highest building in a city determines our sense of the built environment.

When I was growing up in London in the 1970s, the then Post Office Tower was the tallest building in the city, and Centrepoint was the office block which taunted us with its emptiness. In our toilet at home we had a poster of the developer, Harry Hyams, mutating out of the building, the aggressive patterning of his suit merging with the grid of its windows.

Come the 1980s you might have been forgiven for thinking that nothing had changed: the undistinguished Nat West Tower in the City had now become our fixed point of futuristic mediocrity, and still further to the east the Legoland edifice of Canary Wharf taunted us with its cavernous emptiness. Remember that? Occupancy levels of less than 20 per cent, and at the time no prospect of an increase despite tax breaks that would have satisfied an eighteenth-century buccaneer.

Now Canary Wharf taunts us with its plenitude. Despite being the tallest building in the city, there's something about its proportions that seem plump, swollen with enterprise. But even more astonishing is the extent to which the Canary Wharf has defined a new locus for the conurbation.

The London of the Post Office Tower was the London of the North and South Circular Roads; whereas the London of Canary Wharf is the London of the M25. It would be crude to suggest that these buildings are mere ridge poles, thrown up so that a canopy of urbanity can be stretched over them, but in forcing new sight lines on the population they create a different sense of the city's topography.

From the Queen Elizabeth the Second Bridge at Dartford, Canary Wharf is the only really salient point the eye can batten on to, and the same is true of any eastern approach. The city conjured up by this juxtaposition of six-lane motorway and Legoland skyscraper is one of illimitable warehousing and defunct industry; multiplexes and mirrored glass; its car-clogged arteries slashed by more car-clogged arteries.

It would be ludicrous to imagine that we could regain any sense of London as a more intimate environment by introducing Riyadh-style zoning, but it would create a far more credible sense of the polis if our tallest building were in the West End, rather than the Isle of Dogs.

OUT! OUT! BLIND SPOT

In my novel, *My Idea of Fun* (1993) the following lines appear: '[It] was a hideous modernist joke, the prefiguration of 10,000 bypass-bound corporate compounds, the blind people's home, St Dunstan's ... where the vision-crips, the spazzy sightless fumbled their way beneath the cruel-joke edifice. (Can't you just imagine the architect pissing himself with laughter as he shaded in the hideous eaves, ruled the brutal perpendiculars and traced the shaved pubis of the concrete façade! Confident that here at last was a clientele who would be in no position to object to his conception of the modern!)'

For years now they've bothered me. I wrote the novel – intentionally – without going back to the Sussex coastal locations, where I had spent some of my childhood, and which I'd used to form the backdrop to the novel's action. I thought there would be a greater authenticity to my recollections – and therefore fidelity to a child's perception of the world – if I didn't scout them out anew. Naturally, I got a fair amount wrong; one particularly galling mistake was reversing the locations of Saltdean and Peacehaven.

At the time of writing I thought the gag about St Dunstan's was pretty much justified. As a child I remembered it having a fantastically stark aspect. Sited on a chalk cliff top, rearing up out of the bowling-green-short turf, and outlined against the bald hummocks of the South Downs.

Surrounded by small pitch-and-putt golf courses, and accompanied only by the equally massive and lowering Roedean girls' public school, there was little to provide a sense of scale; either St Dunstan's was big – or it was really big. There could be no middle ground.

Last week I went back and took another look. As I suspected, the façade didn't resemble a 'shaved pubis'; there was little in the way of eaves at all, and while the perpendiculars might have been brutal, that was in keeping with the overall style of the building. The real knockout though, was that the building was far older. As a child I'd thought it was a 1960s reprise, when in fact it was a 1930s classic, as important an example of British modernism as the De La Warr Pavilion, up the coast in Bexhill.

When I called a nice Mr Ray Hazan, the PR manager at St Dunstan's, I was soon filled in with the facts. St Dunstan's was designed in 1935 by Francis Lorne, of the St John, Burnett, Tate & Lorne Partnership. It was completed in 1938. The 'aircraft' design of the building – two extending wings leading off a massive, seven-storey glass 'fuselage' – was revolutionary, one of the greatest glass frontages of any building at that time. The kitchens were sited at the top of the building so there would be no dispersal of cooking odours. Then there were those brutal perpendiculars: guide rails provided on all the floors and external walkways.

I asked Mr Hazan if he thought the amount of glass in the frontage was dictated by a desire on the part of Francis Lorne to provide partially sighted inmates with as much natural light as possible. 'I'd love to think that they were that well advanced,' he replied, 'but to be honest we've actually had to work very hard to preserve the building, what with the salt and the sea air here. We've even had a fair amount of corrosion on some internal girders.'

But that being so, the building has been adequately maintained, and changed substantially over the years to match the evolving needs of the blind and the partially sighted. 'Originally,' Mr Hazan said, 'there were dormitories for 20, but now the accommodation is largely bedrooms with *en suite* bathrooms.'

St Dunstan's is a private charity, depending entirely on public donation, they have no government support. Set up to cater for servicemen blinded in the First World War, the charity still aims to provide cradle-to-grave support, training and guidance for the visually handicapped.

Do I feel small about the gag I made in the 1993 novel? You bet your bum. But then there's always Roedean for me to train my acerbic eye on, and in that case I'll hold no quarter.

BRIGHTON ROCKS

In the underground swimming pool of the Metropole Hotel on Brighton's seafront, there's a *trompe l'oeil* mural designed to give you the impression that you're actually swimming in a pool set into the esplanade itself, looking out over the Palace Pier.

Of course, you'd be unlikely to be looking out over the West Pier, not in a hotel mural at any rate. Ever since I can remember – from earliest childhood – Brighton's West Pier has been in slow and steady decline. In the early 1980s this accelerated dramatically, and now all that is left of a once noble piece of Victoriana is a ghost pier, all flaking paint and twisted pieces of protruding iron. The council has now been obliged – because of dangerous incursions on to the unsafe structure – to demolish the landward end of the pier, leaving only a heavily barred walkway.

The pier now resembles a pleasure zone designed for the hereafter. It's not hard to imagine descending into Hades, pitching up at the Styx, and finding that instead of Charon being on hand to make with the oars, you're expected to walk across on the West Pier.

I find it particularly elegiac because, being a child of more than average mawkishness, I always preferred the desultory air of the West Pier to the flashier competitor to the east. (Actually, it wasn't simply mawkishness: one of the great appeals of the West Pier was that you could turn right out of my grandparents' house in Vernon Terrace and proceed straight down the hill and directly on to the pier, without having to make the slightest diversion.) Whereas the Palace Pier was bigger and had better rides, the West Pier had an almost bucolic air.

In the 1960s all the old 'What the Butler Saw' kinetoscopes were still in place: you dropped in a copper cartwheel, turned the handle and gross impropriety – a naked ankle, shoulder, or a pair of giant bloomers – would ensue. Even more anachronistic were the mechanised *tableaux vivants*, which depicted the beheading of Mary Queen of Scots, or the execution of Dr Crippen, the jerky metal figures swinging and chopping in glass-sided cabinets; and once again – all for a penny.

Granted, it was on the West Pier that I first experienced the delights of that utterly novel entertainment – the bouncy castle. This c. 1971 bouncy castle was a primitive thing in which the saltatorial infants were completely enclosed in an inflated plastic membrane, like so many particles in Brownian motion. But it was nothing compared to what the Palace Pier had on offer even then. Its broad end platform allowed for helter-skelters, ghost trains and dodgems. Today it is graced by those astonishing rides wherein adolescents of all ages are thrown into the air strapped to enormous hammers.

This weekend I noted that the new ghost train, which is on the opposite side of the pier from 20 years ago, has been closely modelled on its predecessor. As for the helter-skelter – it's the same one. Standing at the end of the Palace Pier palpable waves of regeneration beat off of the Brighton shingle. Myriad sunbathers studded the shoreline; massed promenaders bought tat. Everywhere you go in the town there are new businesses, bars and shops – the South Coast conurbation has increased in population tenfold in a quarter decade. Not only that, the people are irrepressibly polyglot and, gulp, trendy. They talk of the 'vibe' and the 'action'. This in Brighton and Hove, where about the best action you could have expected in the past was someone dying of a heart attack while watching a game of bowls!

And yet throughout it all the West Pier continues to wither and die. Like someone with a terminal illness sitting among the healthy – a mortal downer. Possibly it should stay that way in order to remind us all of the vanity of imagining, even for a second, that the pursuit of pleasure precedes the retreat from economics.

YOU CAN'T GET THE STAFF NOWADAYS

I've been lying in bed for the past few days, a victim of fatigue, stress, pressure – indeed all of the little erosions of one's confidence that will, eventually, lead to such a comprehensive subsidence. In the long hours I have contemplated life from beneath the sheltering duvet, Lady Bracknell's famous imprecation has never been far from my internal ear: 'Arise sir from that semi-recumbent position!' But alas I cannot arise – I am fatally slumped.

You might have thought that bed was a fairly barren place from which to contemplate the nature of the built environment, but I haven't found it so. In order to save my wife and infant son from waking up three times a night in a pool of paterfamilias sweat, I have moved my lubricious cadaver up to the spare bedroom. Here in the eaves I don't so much toss and turn, as splash and splosh.

I have a fixed-angle view from where I slop, of a small portion of the abutting house. It's no more than a patch of 30 London bricks, with a smear of snotty mortaring, but in my fevered state I can meditate upon it for hours. In part, this is because when I was a child the bed I slept in at my grandparents' house occupied exactly the same position and I had a similar non-view. Not only that, my grandparents' house – a five-storey terrace – was, in terms of layout remarkably similar to the one I currently infest.

Lying in my fevered state I listen to the sounds of people

moving around the gaff, and am transported to my own childhood. Perhaps that isn't Tracey, my son Ivan's minder, sterilising a bottle in the kitchen, but my grandmother's cook Doris, banging the oven door as she removes one of her notorious chocolate cakes? (These cakes were so dense, family myth maintained, that you could see the corner of a piece poking out from your stomach, if you didn't masticate sufficiently before swallowing.) This heavy madeleine opened the floodgates to an innundation of recollection about that Brighton terrace. My brother, the architectural historian, teaches a course called 'The Victorian House'. He bamboozles his MTV-watching students in upstate New York by ponderously informing them at the outset that he himself spent time in a functioning Victorian house when he was a child.

He's exaggerating – but only slightly. The servants' bells may have all been disconnected, but they were still there, attached to the board in Doris' kitchen; as were the discrete, black bell pulls, strategically located by the over-stuffed armchairs in the upstairs drawing room. The old gas brackets were still in many of the rooms. In the portion of the house that my grandparents actually used these had been converted to electroliers, but elsewhere they were merely otiose. All over the house there was this sense of the present as having been worked up out of the objects of the past.

My grandparents had been in staggered retreat within the house's frontiers for some 30 years by the time I got to know it in the 1960s. They occupied the basement (where my grandfather laboured in his library to produce a three-volume work reconciling all religion, philosophy and science); the ground floor (where the redoubtable

Doris laboured to produce meals which would have made suitable foundations for a citadel); and the first floor (where they did no labour, but instead drank 'bombshells' – six parts gin to one of Vermouth – in a not-inelegant drawing room).

But the further reaches of the house were untouched from the time when the retreat – in the face of the unavailability of domestic labour – had been ordered. In the top bedroom the old bed my father slept on in the 1920s was still there: a disturbing, box-like construction which threatened to fold you into itself if you dared to perch on its sideways-retractable mattress. In a nearby cupboard there were my great-grandfather's day books from the 1880s, shortly after the house had been built. These detailed in effortful, copperplate handwriting, the precise expenditures it took to keep this institution-cum-home running.

I was in Brighton the other day and went to see the old house. Not only was it divided up into flats, but on the smoked glass above the front door, the legend 'Sussex House' had been stencilled. It looked older now than it ever had then. But I would feel that way, wouldn't I, lying as I am in a disturbing, box-like construction, and listening to the domestics banging about below.

'I used to live in a shoe – but then I discovered in-line skating ...'

CLIENT HOSPITALITY

I feel saturated with the built environment. I feel as if I've been dashed by pebbles, pumped full of concrete, and maculated with a mastic gun. I want out. I feel as the pseudo-William Wallace character, played by Mel Gibson in the film *Braveheart*, must have felt when he screamed, 'Freedom!', but in my case the freedom I desire is an absence of bricks, mortar, steel, wood … effectively, anything which can be combined or assembled to form a habitable structure.

I can't remember that moment in childhood when I first became aware of how replete with habitation is this country. It was early though. I associate it with my first important intimation of death, which happened when I was around five, in Cromer, north Norfolk. My father, macabre man that he was, had spent much of the day describing the ingurgitation of Dunwich by the North Sea, and extemporising on the soluble nature of the East Anglian coastline. That night as I lay, my hangnails snagging in the Terylene sheets of the B&B, I was visited with a Blakean vision of the entire landmass tipping up on its side like a plate, then slipping into the scummy, washing-up water of the sea.

People, cars, animals, buildings, were all whipped up into a cyclone of matter and despatched holus-bolus. The world returned to flux – or advanced to entropy. It was hell on insurance premiums. I awoke screaming – or perhaps had never slept at all. Ever since then, I have been hypersensitive to the way human presence has informed the land. By my teens too much country walking with the same macabre, town-planner *manqué,* led me to appreciate that if you wanted to see anything approaching a 'natural' landscape in Britain, you were as well advised to stick your head inside a thicket in Rainham, Kent as tramp across a grouse moor.

Yet the spectacle of urban decay in our inner cities, in 1999, still moves me to suggest that we may have reached a new nadir of clutter. I was in Manchester last week, staying at a swish new morgue of a hotel called Malmaison. This modern menhir occupies a prime location on the shoulder of the road which debouches from the station into Piccadilly itself. It's a site which had long been a vacant gulch of mud and vetch. I think I recall seeing a prostitute service a client there about five years ago, when I was dashing to an early train. Nice to think they can check into the hotel now and do it on sheets.

I've spent long nights wandering the bombed-out inner areas of Manchester. There's something about the sheer extent and relentlessness of the urban blight which draws me back in again and again. In Manchester you can now wander from estate to estate to high rise; in and out of entire districts which have sufficient numbers of burnt, bombed, gutted, and abandoned properties, that they've become ghost towns. It's the same on Tyneside and in parts of the Black Country.

I know I'm always ranting on at you constructors to get out on your feet and rub noses with the built environment, but in the week which sees the publication of Richard

Rogers's vital new programme for urban regeneration, you have to admit that it's time we took a less than academic view of the issues. Or so I felt, lying in my vast bed at Malmaison, listening to the sough of the night-time city outside, and watching a *Newsnight* debate on urban regeneration, including some prime footage of the very mean streets I'd just been wandering.

Yup, it was all very well getting the camera out yet again and trotting around streets of boarded-up, but perfectly recoverable housing. It was well worth hearing what the few remaining residents had to say about the constant threat to their lives and properties, but none of it will amount to anything more than a quantity surveyor's imagination, if it isn't matched with money. Our cities are rotting because we've axed the principle of municipal housing, and allowed income differentials to increase. That's all.

Oh, and one last thing. If you lot spend several hours wandering around this contemporary legacy of Ozymandias, this shattered visage of a city, I wager you'll be considerably less hortatory publicly, about what you're slapping up on the outskirts.

'Mr dear fellow – this is folly!'

DUNDROWNING

I saw an item on the news the other night about a rather beautiful Georgian folly that was about to fall off the cliffs of Derry in Northern Ireland. The folly is a two-storey, domed rotunda, and the cliff it sits upon is being reinforced with steel rods. The cost!, you might exclaim – so much better to build one's follies on more provident ground.

The item stirred in me the memory of so many other structures, so improvidently sited. When I was a child we holidayed near Dunwich in Suffolk. My father never tired of telling me how the whole town had slid into the North Sea, during a particularly savage storm in the eleventh century. In one night of innundation, Dunwich went from being the biggest city in East Anglia – boasting 12 churches, fine walls and a monastery – to being the sleepy little village it is now. It is said that on a stormy night you can still hear the church bells ringing in the depths.

But it wasn't only in the past that people indulged in such quixotic construction. I have a friend who has a shack on the shingle beach at Dungeness. All day long he is troubled by two nuisances. One is the hordes who come to worship – and sometimes desecrate – the marvellous garden that the late Derek Jarman, the film director, created outside his shack. The other is the continual rumble of lorries carrying shingle from one side of the promontory on which the Dungeness nuclear power station stands, then dumping it on the other side. This is because the power station was sited on the side of the promontory that is steadily being eroded by the sea. Nutty, you might say, and it certainly is.

But no nuttier that the spectacle of the gleaming new Getty Museum in Santa Monica, California. This triumphal building – a series of the most graceful concrete arabesques and glass furbelows – is, predictably enough, more or less smack on top of the San Andreas Fault. Setting loss of life, property and livelihood to one side, there's a certain grim enjoyment to the notion that this most miserly of men is likely to have the quintillions of his crazed bequest instantaneously destroyed.

Nobody wishes to be 'likened unto a foolish man, which built his house upon the sand', but I can't help feeling that there's more to this than meets the eye. Just as a child labours to construct a sand castle, then delights in kicking it precipitately to pieces before the tide comes in, so I can't help feeling the desire of adults to pit their constructions against the elements is a necessary – and indeed essential – part of building ambition.

MEGADEATH MANSIONS

As a teenager, I spent the long hot summer of 1976 walking in the Welsh hills. One day we camped by a valley which had recently been flooded to provide a reservoir to cool a nuclear power station. This humming behemoth crouched on the ill-defined shore, looking like the headquarters of an alien expeditionary force. The lines of fence posts disappearing into the blue-green waters; the isolated spire in the middle of the expanse, marking the site of an abandoned village; and the unnatural warmth of the water which had rubbed up against megadeath; all conspired to give the place a sublime atmosphere.

In the night we swam out into the reservoir, acutely aware of the submerged territory beneath our dabbling feet. It was a moonlit night, but in addition we had the halogen-bathed power station to act as a beacon. The sheer size of the thing made its architectural merits superfluous. This could suck in the elements; and in its concrete heart elemental transmogrifications were taking place. It would be the most pathetic of fallacies to remark on form in view of this terrifying substance.

Over the years I have retained my ambivalence to these most threatening and exhilarating of structures.

My most enduring affair with a nuclear power station has been with Sizewell in Suffolk, where I lived for nearly two years. I knew the old station – Sizewell A – as a child, when we used to take family holidays on this coast. It presents a most austere face to the North Sea: a weathered oblong of concrete, some hundreds of feet high and wide. Bizarrely, the mullions of its vast, multi-paned oblong windows suggest domesticity, as if this Brobdingnagian building had inhabitants – possibly to scale.

And as if this weren't enough, they've now built a new, fast-breeder reactor – Sizewell B – right next to A. This is housed inside a white dome, roughly one-and-a-half times the size of St Paul's. A dome made from a glowing ceramic substance. A dome which crouches on top of an enormous, blue, subtly iridescent plinth over 300 metres in length.

When I lived in the area I would often walk out at night, within the humming zone of the two reactors. Pressing on along the beach, eventually I would escape their grave bulk, and find myself striding with the sea to my right and the whispering reed marshes of Minsmere bird reserve to my left. The juxtaposition between the bulk of high technology on the one hand, and the flimsiness of nature on the other, always evoked that awe-full feeling I first had some 20 years earlier.

I don't think that anything environmentalists can say to persuade us of the dangers of the technology these buildings house, will ever entirely offset the awe we feel when contemplating them. As it is to nuclear power stations, so it is to all the metallic immensities of the fossil-fuel industries; the rigs and refineries, gasometers and terminals. Only if these were treated as potentially ergonomic structures would the spell they cast be broken. Paradoxically, if their creators attempted to humanise them, we would see them for the anti-human things they are.

'If you're amenable I'd like to develop your cloudfield site …'

A DARK VIEW OF GAY HILLS

At the Chateau Marmont, on Los Angeles' notorious Sunset Boulevard, I lie on my bed and stare out at a scene of total bucolia. A steep hill mounts up behind the hotel grounds; a hill that's a riot of sub-tropical verdancy. In among the palms and perennials, are studded ochre-tiled roofs of mock-Italianate, mock-Hispanic and mock-just-about-everything-else villas. The sky is blue, the scents agreeably pungent.

But the soundtrack for this experience of enchanted *rus in urbe* is distinctly disconcerting. A cacophonous chorus of whooping and screaming police – and other emergency service vehicles' – sirens. Not just one or two, but maybe ten or fifteen of them are reducing me to a state of quivering anticipation: What's going on? Another earthquake? Another riot? Independence Day?

None of the above; it's simply another very ordinary day on Sunset Boulevard. For, while the back end of the hotel exhibits a sense of gentle repose that sets mock-baronial building and lush gardens in agreeable counterpoint, the façade of the Chateau Marmont confronts a six-lane highway (the Boulevard), where the action is continuous. At night the prostitutes prowl, and the drug dealers drive by. We're not far from the Viper Room and other notorious haunts of Los Angeles' *jeunesse dorée*, the so-called 'Gen-Xers'. These youths are shinily encapsulated by their wealth, and there are so many of them that they spill off the wide sidewalks on to the road, forming a crowd of trust funding.

Yet, turn off the Boulevard in a southerly direction and within yards you are among houses that for sheer, bland suburbanity can't be beat. Large bungalows are set in green plots. Some of them have diamond-mullioned windows, some have decorative wooden shutters, hasped and hinged with cast iron. The road flows down the hill towards central Los Angeles for many miles. The Los Angeles conurbation is astonishingly vast. Within the black district there's a hill-bound suburb dubbed the 'Black Hollywood', and there's a range of gay hills: Silverlake.

When you go to visit a friend it's common to get on the freeway and drive for five or even ten exits. The network of freeways within the greater Los Angeles area has the same scope as the entire arterial road system of south-east England.

But as you zip by in your car, the fact that it's hard to differentiate between its districts, and the peculiar pastiche of Los Angeles' architecture (everything looks like something else), become aspects of the same phenomenon: an urban environment running amok for the millennium.

It sounds dreadful, but it's also incredibly invigorating.

'They may look like incomprehensible lines on the desert floor now – but wait until we put the meters in …'

YOU COULDN'T MAKE IT UP

It's autumn so it must be Booker Prize time. People think that this is a significant literary prize: in terms of sales, prestige – posterity even. It goes without saying that the probity of the judges is beyond question – yet there is one crushing piece of prejudice which has prevented at least one British author winning the prize in recent years. I refer to Tim Parks, whose novel (the name of which I cannot, I confess, remember, even though I read it*) undoubtedly deserved the laurels on offer in 1997. I can reveal here, exclusively, the reason why victory eluded Parks: his name. 'Tim Parks is such a negative name,' more than one member of the jury vouchsafed to me, 'if only he'd use the *nom de plume* "Tim Drives". That has real panache. If he'd displayed such confidence in himself we wouldn't have given it to the pretty Indian lady.'

There's something about parking – even the most committed driver seldom has a good word to say about it. Have you ever heard a friend remark of their new auto: 'It's a beauty to handle tight up against the kerb. A little dab on the accelerator, the softest pump on the brakes, a mere stroke at the wheel, and ... *voila!* I find myself perfectly parallel, even when there are only centimetres to fore and aft.'

In Australia, where I had the good fortune to take my

* *Europa*, Secker & Warburg.

driving test, parallel parking is an essential skill. If you can't park within eight inches of the kerb with your first cut – you're out. This is a tad ironic given that Australia is such a vast and empty quarter, but at least it inculcates in drivers the need to know their vehicles' widths, something missing all too often among the drivers on this tiny roundabout we inhabit. Missing along with any sense of proportion when it comes to planning where to put our life-size toy cars once we've stopped playing with them.

I've just received a communication from the London Borough of Lambeth in which they invite my response to their plans to introduce 'new parking controls for Stockwell': yellow lines, residents' permits and metered parking. Included is a handy map of the area along with several paragraphs of astonishing doublethink on the subject. On one side of the brochure they employ white-out-of-blue type to assert that: 'Lambeth is not alone in trying to tackle these problems and together with other agencies is working hard to improve the quality of public transport services available to our residents.' But on the other side of the brochure traditional black-on-white tells a more paranoid story: 'The introduction of controlled parking in neighbouring areas [results] in some people using streets in your area as a free car park to avoid buying a permit where they live.'

To the barricades! We cannot allow this thrust for *lebensraum* by the fascist expansionists in neighbouring areas. We must submit ourselves to this domino logic, which means that the London Borough of Lambeth will, ineluctably, accrue more and more revenue; while we, the rate payers, have less and less to show for it. I've never lived anywhere in London where the introduction of parking controls has resulted in an end to parking congestion. Once and for all, boroughs are all connected to each other! Push down on the boil at one point, and the pus just emerges somewhere else.

There is conceivably a future in which commuters and carriage-trade interlopers have all been priced out of the parking-space market in inner London – and its main suburban centres, some of which, such as Hampstead, have the most draconian controls in the known universe – leaving the leafy avenues and breezy boulevards deliciously voided. Residents' permits in this glorious new city-wide car park will be astronomical, since – as every permit parker knows – they increase in direct proportion to the extent of the area in which said controls operate.

Like so many other aspects of urban planning, it appears that parking controls are in essence iatrogenic, that is, a disease created by those who profess to cure it. The truth is always so much more awful and grim than fiction.

'He isn't dead – he's protesting …'

MULTIPLEX OF MIDDENS

When the Crystal Palace burnt to the ground in 1936, the streets of the surrounding districts, Sydenham and Norwood, ran with molten glass. As nice an apotheosis of the great age of glass and iron construction as one could wish to imagine. It was a spectacular fire, with explosions throwing jets of molten debris high into the skies of night time, south London suburbia.

The summit of the hill where the Palace stood has remained free of redevelopment, until now. Plans are currently under consideration to build a multiplex cinema on the corner of the old site, adjacent to where the telecommunications mast spears its iron way aloft.

A multiplex! I ask you. A particularly unloving piece of development when you consider that this is the major eminence of south London, the corresponding bookend to the hills of Hampstead and Highgate to the north of the Thames valley. Looking north from the site you have the whole raddled ocean of London, bluer and greyer; and to the south before you the vast succession of suburb-upon-park-upon-suburb, stretching away to house an infinity of Mr Pollys, all the way to eternity – or at any rate Bromley.

And if, in a city noted for its lack of prospects, the appeal to a real panorama isn't enough to sway entrepreneurs, planning bureaucrats and the public, there's the Palace itself to consider. An enormous, cruciform construction, all that remains is the overgrown foundation, the descending terraces and the riddle of the balustrades surmounted by sphinxes. But despite the overgrown shrubbery and the usual debris of park life, there's still a grandeur about the crunchy gravel paths and the stairways furred with lichen.

The site is a fitting size: in proportion to the city that flows around it. More than that; the site is a fine entrée to the park with its pocket punch bowl, pedalo lagoon, and concrete dinosaurs stalking the rhododenrons.

When I visited it the other week I was in search not of *temps perdu*, but a protestors' camp set up to combat the curse of the summer blockbuster. I asked several strollers whether they knew where it was, but they were unforthcoming. Eventually, a man mowing the rectangle of grass where once the fruits of the world's largest empire were displayed, directed me a gap in the fence leading to the early Anglo-Saxon period.

It's difficult to say whether the sartorial affectations of the eco-warriors determine their building styles, or *vice versa*. Perhaps the relationship is one of function rather than causality: it's convenient if you're living in a bender, or a tree-borne platform to wear loose tunics and pantaloons gathered at the ankle. Suffice to say, that's what the few desultory types mooching around the camp had on.

This protestors' camp was mostly ground based – though there may have been tunnels beneath. A lookout tower arose from the corrugated-iron perimeter fence, giving the impression that the camp was an organic development. The rest of the structures were bender-cum-humpies. Plank or earth floors, half walls of board, roofed with tarpaulins or sheets of canvas stretched over poles. At other

protest camps I've visited the dwellings have been platforms hoisted up into the tree canopy, which imparts a certain novelty and even elegance of construction, but here at
Crystal Palace the feel of the settlement was resolutely
Bronze Age, right down to the middens.

The idea that in some distant future Crystal Palace
might be excavated, revealing successively: the remains of
a Bronze Age hill fort; the remains of a multiplex cinema;
the remains of an iron and glass palace; and then far far
deeper the remains of another Bronze Age hill fort, brings
a twitch to my jowls.

Will the disputatious archeologists of the distant future
be led to posit an interregnum, a dark age between their
civilisation and our own? I certainly hope so, for the history of the built environment is never as straightforward
as we might like to imagine, and progress is a crooked
path through dusty undergrowth, festooned with con-
doms. I think.

SAVE THE BURGER

'Five miles out of London on the Western Avenue/It must have been a wonder when it was brand new …' So sung Elvis Costello, in the days when his concerns were chiefly architectural. I'm being facetious, but every time I pass the Hoover Factory it does occur to me to wonder whether or not Costello sees its recent, glistening refurbishment, as in any way a product of his protest song?

Certainly the Hoover Factory has been restored to a pristine condition, but I wonder if it is the 'wonder' it must have been when it was brand new? Because, the hard fact of the matter is that far from being the global headquarters for the production of *the* domestic labour-saving device of the twentieth century, the building is now home to Tescos the food retailers.

Not that I have anything against Tescos you understand (though once you discover the company is so-called because it's named after one 'Tessa Cohen' it certainly changes your view). It's just that the conversion of a manufacturing space into a commercial one is never going to be entirely comfortable.

The Hoover factory, with its Parthenon-like proportions, its soaring pediment, its elevation of the notion of the fan light to celestial lumesence, is a very temple of manufacture. Just as the noblemen of the Middle Ages built their palaces along the Thames, in a line stretching between the material power of the City, and the temporal authority of Westminster, so the noble manufacturers built their palaces along the arterial roads leading out of London, their location and their character denoting their place in the great, economic scheme of things.

My childhood was dominated by numerous seemingly interminable, halting progressions around the North Circular Road. It's mind-boggling now, but in the days before the M25, drivers really did believe that the North Circular constituted a potential saving in journey time – I kid you not. The hours spent squinting through grey haze at factory premises may not have done much for my faith in the car, but it did convert me to these soon-to-be-converted premises.

I loved the Hoover factory, which in the late 1960s and early 1970s had become little more than a greying, flaking hulk. But once we turned east along the North Circular from Hangar Lane (now blessed with a 'gyratory system', but then little more than a roundabout) there was a whole series of grand factories. My favourite was the Gross Cash Registers factory. This was pretty much the same shape as the late, lamented Bankside Power Station – a tall central tower, flanked by two 'wings' of equal extent. What distinguished it was its dazzling whiteness, and the letters G R O S S, inscribed vertically on the tower.

But just as Britain has ceased to be the workshop of the world, so our industrial architecture has declined accordingly. Nowadays the best bet for an architect concerned with designing such premises, is for her to coat the exterior of the building with a reflective material, in the vain hope that there will be something nearby that looks a little better. And anyway, industrial buildings, whether for manufacture or anything else, are now usually confined with those of their own ilk, banged up in ghettos called industrial estates (I like the echo of feudalism implicit in this).

I don't know what happened to Gross Cash Registers – presumably they went the way of all Hoover flesh. At any rate you no longer see their tills at the till, and the building is long gone too. In our current economy, founded as it is on providing 'retail services' to the rest of the world – rather than things that they might be able to retail or consume – there is no need for such buildings. Instead the arterial roads which course out of our cities can be graced with structures that adequately reflect the icy heart of cool Britannia.

Why worry that the Hoover factory has been turned into a giant Tescos, when just back down the road a way, there's the atrocity exhibition of 'Office World'; and right next to it the flame-grilled certainty of a drive through the hell of Burger King? Go on Elvis, see if you can manage to pen a protest song about that one!

'It may not be what it's meant for – but it does the trick!'

THE DETAIL'S DETAIL

My wife's favourite building in the world is the Glasgow School of Art, designed by Charles Rennie Mackintosh – and it's easy to see why. Never, to my mind, has a single building so clearly exhibited an exciting union of form and function. We went to see it the other day, stopping first at another Rennie Mackintosh building, The Willow Tree Tea Rooms on Sauchiehall Street. ('Sauchie' means 'willow' in Gaelic – not a lot of people know that.)

The Tea Rooms are a sliver of elegance pinioned between later conversions and marooned on an arid stretch of pedestrian precinct. They were opened in 1904 and until 1926 were a fashionable rendezvous for Glaswegian tea-heads. Unfortunately, after their closure the premises became a department store, and hardly any of the original fittings and decorations survived the transition. The current occupants, M M Harrison, a jewellers', have painstakingly restored the interior, complete with gesso panels, bas reliefs, and ubiquitous willow motifs; but this apparent sympathy is savagely undercut by the fact that most of the stuff they sell is reproduction Rennie Mackintosh.

This makes a stunning commercial premises seem strangely bogus, as the Rennie Mackintosh style is itself oddly proleptic: an anticipation of Bauhausian rationality, late modernism and retro-puritanism, refracted through the darkening glass of the *belle époque*. That being noted, a lot of these Mackintosh-clone artefacts are perfectly pleasing to the eye; and once you've taken a long look at them to register the key elements of his decorative style, you begin to recognise its influence everywhere you go in Glasgow.

But before doing that I went round the art school. I'd seen bits of this beautiful whale of a building before – usually when travelling at speed in cars full of carousers – but I'd never seen it complete and in the raw light of day. What a piece of work! It was a *coup de foudre*. A perfect synecdoche of a structure – part reflecting whole and whole part. I particularly like the way the building blankets the steep hill it sits on, embracing it with its foundations. There's that, and there's also the way each fluid bow of rendering is contained with a rectilinear frame, so that classical and modern continually check one another.

Then there are the details. The lamp brackets ranged along the fence like Van de Graaff generators waiting to be activated; the finials of the fence itself, the iron crescents and hoops of which resemble astrolabes; and the magnificent main door plates, which spell out 'Art School'. Then there's the details' detail. Adorning the façade of the art school are three external buttresses, tilting out over the local void, comprised of two struts subtending one another.

While not 'functional' in the strictest sense, the buttresses certainly do serve a function. For it is the Rennie Mackintosh details that have fissioned all over the built environment of Glasgow: these arrangements of austere lines into partial graticules; these pairings of oblique – and obscure – extensors, which may be flowers or fabrications; and those implants of minute squares of mirroring into much larger areas of the translucent.

Anywhere you go in Glasgow you'll happen across Mackintoshesque detailing, whether it's a fan light in a door, or a paling in a fence, or – in the case of the Ubiquitous Chip, where we had dinner – just about everything. Glasgow is a handsome city, but I'm not entirely certain that Mackintosh is quite the architect it deserves. He could be said to represent a paradoxical relationship, as an artist of genius, with his Clydeside culture. The same kind of paradox that's evinced by the example of Shakespeare in England.

KERB-VAULTING

As Levi-Strauss so sagely remarked: '... the intrinsic value of a small-scale model is that it compensates for the renunciation of sensible dimensions by the acquisition of intelligible ones.' Oh that Claude! What a way he had with words; I don't doubt that he was more or less incapable of making other than sagacious remarks. Even nonce phrases such as 'At the end of the day' probably acquired a gnomic penumbra when they issued from his highly structured mouth.

But what he draws our attention to here is something which the built environment, insofar as it allows itself to be defined by the car, almost always exemplifies. It doesn't matter how many pedestrian precincts we lay out, or how many quartiers of street-front habitations we put down, when these acts of zoning are themselves predicated on a large-scale model which entirely renounces the intelligible in favour of the sensible.

By this I mean exactly what is implied by Freddie Ayer's famous answer, when he was asked which single thing he found most evocative of Paris. 'A road sign,' the great logical positivist replied 'with "Paris" written on it.' Ayer was remarking on the bare-bones epistemology of his own philosophy, but I think he signposts our way towards a future in which an underpass on the Periphérique has more significance than the Faubourg St Germain. Oops! We're there already.

To complete my trio of Built Environment Aphorisms (soon to be published as a daringly etiolated volume by the Edifice Press), we would do well to bring to mind Lewis Mumford, stuffed with sagacity as the man was. Indeed, it was often said during Mumford's own lifetime, that if you thoroughly seasoned him, rubbed him with olive oil, and popped him in the oven at gas mark six for an hour-and-a-half, there would be no requirement for any additional stuffing at all. Anyway, Mumford said, or wrote, or perhaps simply implied through odour, that: 'In the city time is made visible.'

Now, all these remarks are, bizarrely, by way of introducing you to my new form of transport, the Go-Ped Bigfoot. I normally never give commercial endorsement of any kind whatsoever – it is anathema to anyone who isn't a toady on a cosmic level – but I have to say that the Bigfoot wins my unreserved admiration. Anyway I'm confident that should Go-Ped manage to sell enough of them, restrictions on their use – they currently occupy a legislative grey area – would effectively cap the market.

The Go-Ped, as its deliriously generic name implies, is an old-fashioned, sit-up-and-beg scooter, with a 22cc petrol engine tacked on the back. Full throttle the thing will manage about 20 mph on a good, flat straight. Not that the flat straight is what you should – or can – reasonably ride the mini-beast on. No, the Bigfoot is not a means of transport, it's a toy for people who want to do miniature scrambling. (There are other powered scooters, but the Bigfoot is the only one I've seen which advertises itself as having an off-road capability.) If you do choose to drive the thing in the city you have to employ a mixture of human and engine

'I understand he farms bonsai on a nearby allotment ...'

power in order to avoid the unwanted attentions of the Old Bill; outraged older citizenry; and potentially violent, mocking or admiring young lads. The Go-Ped isn't cool on pavements which are anything more than sparsely tenanted, roadways the same.

Interestingly, this drives the rider into a relationship with the city which is novel and provocative. Debarred from the conventional routes prescribed either by the planner, or the oxen-like tread of history-herded humanity, the go-pedder is free to view the built environment anew.

Yes, I have become a voyager in the interstices of the city, in its profoundly interzonal hinterlands. I wouldn't deny for a second that two feet are perfectly adequate for exploring these regions, but there's something about the absurdity of the Go-Ped (most people simply burst out laughing when I pass by on it), and its deliciously ironic, post-modern take on the notion of motor transport, which make it a fantastic platform from which to survey 'time made visible'.

My television documentary, 'One Man's Go-Ped to Birmingham', will be appearing on Channel 4 in the autumn. The accompanying book *Travels on My Go-Ped* is published by the Edifice Press. Donald Sinden is currently recording a talking-book version aimed at the humour-impaired.

XL

SEEING RED

'If you have been wondering why central London is grid-locked ... here is the reason,' reads the headline on page 19 of the *Evening Standard* and the article goes on to tell us that – according to the RAC – the closure of the Mall for resurfacing will cost the capital £3.5 million over the 12-week period. Apparently cabbies are netting a cool £100,000 a day extra in fares, which is presumably why they look so chipper about the ongoing congestion when they're interviewed on regional television news. Actually, the thought that these stout yeomen of Essex are clawing in such a humungous bounty purely because some over-weight bureaucrats can't face waddling across St James's Park, almost makes the whole thing worthwhile.

Anyway, why should we listen to the *Evening Standard*, which, of course, is not really a newspaper at all? Indeed, there's something particularly noisome about the attention which the editor gives to covering transport stories in this coagulated metropolis (in the same issue there's a tendentious leader lambasting unionised tube workers for 'holding the capital to ransom'), when the publication he's editing will barely sustain you the length of two average tube stops. I've often succeeded in reading it still quicker by adopting the simple expedient of only reading articles about 'reality' and not the theatre, film, Andrew Lloyd Webber etc.

It isn't the hike in cab fares that bothers the *Standard* anyway, and nor is it the fact that the concierge at the Ritz is having to tell guests to 'expect long delays'. The causal reality behind the jams is that the Royal Parks Agency, which has responsibility for maintaining the Mall, was under no obligation to formally co-ordinate their plans with any of the other agencies responsible for maintaining London's roads. The agency did gain approval from the Culture Secretary (the permanently prolix Mr Chris Smith), as well as passing its plans on to Westminster Council and the Metropolitan Police, out of consideration.

The agency tells us that to complete the work any quicker they would have needed to pay workers double time (My God! Totally unacceptable!); and that to leave one lane open would've increased the cost of the £1 million project substantially as well. So, tough titty all you stranded motorists, you can't possibly expect the royals to dig that deep for redoing their driveway, which, for the vast majority of the year they quite happily let us play on with our toy vehicles.

I am one of those toy vehicle drivers, because it just so happens that the Mall is on my school run. As a result, my eldest son has always maintained that Buck House is a fairly modest *estaminet*. One he himself wouldn't mind inhabiting at a point in the near future. Nauseating stuff. The journey as the crow flies from where I live (Vauxhall), to where my older children go to school (Hammersmith), goes nowhere near any royal parks, but such is the queered reality of mass human behaviour, that it's quicker, during the rush hour, for us to take a counterintuitive route. Heading initially into the centre of London, we then swing round the side of Hyde Park, and find ourselves – charged with an unearthly momentum – travelling in the opposite direction to prevailing traffic flows, as we carom down the Bayswater Road, Holland Park Avenue and all points west. Now, we'll find ourselves, for the next three weeks, bogged down in the Ultima Thule of the Royal Borough of Kensington and Chelsea, our frail vessel constantly and savagely being cut up by women in nine-series Volvos, wearing sleeveless anoraks and Laura Ashley headscarves. And people say contemporary writing isn't infused with any real sense of suffering!

Though everything they write in the *Standard* is true, they didn't bother to mention why this resurfacing work, over a relatively short stretch of road, should take so long in the first place. The answer is because it's going to be red. That's right, red, like a carpet. Geddit? The Mall is red. And it's rendered red by using special tar and, in place of the standard gear, specially groovy granite chippings from a remote, pink, Welsh quarry. I daresay each of these will be lovingly pressed into the warm surface by an equerry. The whole farce makes me see it already.

Fig. 1 The God Khnum spin-doctoring Egypt, 1800 BC.

WHEN YOU'RE ALONE IN YOUR HEAD

There's nothing lightweight or fatuous about seeking to get an adequate definition of the term 'civilisation'. Everyone ought to have an idea of what's meant by this, unless they prefer to spend their days cantering over the steppes of Central Asia. But for members of the architectural and allied professions to be ignorant of the total context within which they labour – 'civilisation' in its broadest sense – is disturbing in the extreme.

Julian Jaynes, in his epochal work *The Origin of Consciousness and the Breakdown of the Bicameral Mind* defines civilisation thus: 'the art of living in towns of such size that everyone does not know everyone else.' This is not obvious. Certainly it is hardly through our unconsciousness of the activities of our fellow urbanites that we seek to label ourselves 'civilised'. Take the current debacle over the Jubilee Line (one readers may feel has been a slow train coming; but which, nonetheless, to the laity is a positive rocket of unexpectedness), no one thinks that it is our personal ignorance of the electricians involved in the dispute that's slowed the work; or exposed the under- and over-estimates of the tender.

On the contrary, we take it as read that everything will be a lot more 'civilised', if only we can identify at a personal level with the problems involved. Not so. In fact, if we believe Jaynes, humans have been living for many

many millennia in large cities without there being much in the way of conscious communication between them at all. Let alone empathy. According to Jaynes: 'our contemporary religious and city architecture is partly, I think, the residue of our bicameral past. The church or temple or mosque is still called the House of God. In it, we still speak to the god, still bring offerings to be placed on a table or altar before the god or his emblem.'

By 'bicameral', he means, very literally, a mind with two houses. It's Jaynes's contention that up until approximately 1200 BC, humankind, rather than manifesting the kind of reflective self-consciousness we have today, behaved in response to auditory hallucinations, voices which came from the other half – the second house – of their brains. While initially, primitive man may have experienced such 'voices' as the admonitory counsel of ancestors and even recently deceased relatives, over time they came to be identified with the will of the gods, and organised into complex, hierarchical systems.

It's quite a contention: that the ancient civilisations of the Fertile Crescent, the Indus Valley, the Nile and Mesoamerica, were all the creation of non-conscious humans, caused to raise elaborate pyramids, ziggurats and other megaliths in response to an internalised set of commands. Jaynes goes still further, arguing that this ubiquitous city plan – the houses of the populace organised around the larger house of the absent god-king – is, in and of itself, a mnemonic intended to provoke such hallucinatory commands.

Still, to come back to the current Jubilee Line debacle, I can't help thinking that Jaynes must be right. That our very concept of 'civilisation' as inherently self-conscious and rational is what is to blame here. If we understood the Line's construction to be the very embodiment of our collective will, we'd be down there under the Thames ourselves, digging away for all we are worth. Even when London's modern infrastructure was put in place (let's not forget the 200 miles-odd of deep-level tunnels dug before the First World War), the populace still believed in the existence of a civilisation which was embodied by the city. This is no longer the case.

And yet now we are asked to bend our backs to the common weal and support the idea that our civilisation's highest attainment (and I'm talking Millennium Dome here) is an enormous temple within which humanoid effigies reside; a temple clearly designed so as to provoke auditory hallucinations. Well, I think we could all accept that there was a rationality to our vast – and civilised – economies of scale, when some genuine, material benefit was incurred by them; but this is an irrational piece of calendric monumentalism to rival the Nazca lines of Peru.

Which leaves the electricians still in dispute, the Jubilee Line uncompleted and civilisation still in disarray. But if you seriously thought it was going to be any better than this – you must've been hearing voices in your head.

THE ARCHITECT OF A BELLY

What sort of apartment does a sex symbol live in? That's the question which was bedevilling me as I jetted towards Italy the other morning, to interview Ilona Staller (a.k.a. 'La Cicciolina'; or, in English 'Little Dumpling'), the Hungarian-Italian porn actress, whose escapades include serving as a Radical Party member of the Italian parliament, and marrying Jeff Koons, the kitschy American conceptual artist.

The answer is – a very nice one. On a long suburban road which leads out of Rome to the north, Cicciolina's block was just that: a collection of grooved concrete boxes, all piled atop one another in such a way as to provide numerous small balcony and terrace areas, accessed by sliding glass doors. With its imposing railings, private swimming pool, and CCTV intercom system, the apartment block must have been *le dernier cri* a couple of decades ago. Now that the concrete has weathered and fissured, and the railings have tarnished, the corpse of William Holden wouldn't look out of place in the swimming pool. I'm afraid much the same could said about the Little Dumpling.

Christ! If only she *had* been a little dumpling – I could've happily eaten her. Although our interview was scheduled for lunchtime, I knew better than to expect any actual food to materialise. I intended spending a couple of hours with her, then cabbing into the city to sample some pasta and some architecture – in that order. So, as the superannuated sex symbol trilled on and on and on, I could feel my stomach inflating in anticipation of being solidly concreted.

It doesn't matter how far we may have travelled in this world, we still have the crassest of expectations about visiting new places. I'd never been to the Eternal City before, and although I kept telling myself not to anticipate anything in particular, I assumed that my cab ride into town would take me over the Tiber; around Trajan's Column; and through the Coliseum, before depositing me neatly in a dear little trattoria right on top of the Palatine Hill. Instead there was kilometre upon kilometre of choked traffic, retail outlets, low-rise apartment blocks and not-much-higher rise offices. I knew that Rome was built on seven hills, but my cab driver seemed intent on sticking to the valleys. At the very least I'd hoped for incongruous, split-second sights of classical sites in among the twentieth-century travelogue – but no such luck. We did cross the Tiber, but on what appeared to be a reproduction Roman bridge.

Then we were speeding through older, narrower and more crowded streets. Small squares opened out to right and to left; there was a familiar sign depicting two golden arches under the legend 'Pantheon MacDonalds 500m'. We turned in the direction of the pointing arrows, and twenty seconds later I was standing in front of the majestic building itself.

The Pantheon. Wow! The great–granddaddy of all domes. The dome at the beginning of time. I wandered, awed, into its immense concavity, only to discover that the interior really felt rather homely. It could have been the patrolling phalanxes of Benelux exchange students; it could have been the warm September sun streaming in through the oculus; or perhaps it was the way the structure finessed mono- and polytheism – whatever. Suffice to say that for a while my pangs faded, and I was free to experience the best-preserved edifice of ancient Rome.

For a while – but not for long. After all, as Horace remarked: '*Est modus in rebus, sunt certi denique fines / Quos ultra citraque nequit consistere rectum*', and it was getting on for four in the afternoon. If I didn't eat soon I was going to collapse. The Pantheon wasn't helping either; for what did the building resemble, with its immense cylindrical core, and its vast dome, but a huge, boomingly empty belly? I staggered off in search of pasta.

There were no wheaten noodles to be had. Here, there and everywhere tables had been cleared and chairs tipped back; there would be no more *mangare* until sundown. On and on I limped through the centre of Rome, like some low-rent Marcello Mastrionani searching for yummy Anita Ekberg. Eventually, I had to retrace my steps and seek out those two profoundly non-triumphal golden arches. 'Make mine a Big Pantheon and fries,' I told the bemused Clearasil-user behind the counter 'and make it snappy – I haven't eaten in an eternity.'

O most noble Caesar – the Senate has dedicated two triumphal arches to you!

I ❤ THE M25

I'm still monumentally exercised by the interface between transport and the built environment. Oh, that and PFIs. The government answer to everything is a PFI – in fact, the government is the PFI Friday show. From now on everything is going to paid for by these handy examples of infrastructure on the never-never. The rail system is going to be given a makeover, ditto the London tube system, and of course, more roads. Lots. Not as many, doubtless, as many would like, but lots of them.

I was at the Houses of Parliament yesterday, interviewing Margaret Beckett, the president of the council, leader of the House, member of the great and the good, etc. etc. I asked her how, in particular, the current impasses on transport policy relate to environmental damage and whether she thought they should be resolved by firm government action: bans on private vehicles in the city centre; restrictions on private cars generally; improved (and genuinely public-sector) funding for alternatives. You get the picture. She thought for a while and then began: 'You have to take a balanced view …' And I knew she'd lost me.

There's nothing remotely balanced about a situation which drives a perfectly sane individual such as myself to piloting a tiny motorised skateboard around a metropolis. Yet, were it not for my vagabond Go-Pedding I fear I'd go tonto. The current level of closures (the Northern Line from Kennington to Moorgate, the entire Circle Line) on the London tube system means it can become fatally overloaded should further failures occur. Which they inevitably do. In the clotted, fume-tangy months of mid-summer, London traffic can reach baroque levels of confusion. This ludicrous screw-up in replacing metal-fatigued girders (the Circle Line), and upgrading track so trains can run at the speeds they were designed for 40 years ago (the Northern Line), means that before long we'll be carving holes in the smog in order to get room to breathe.

In the past week I've employed taxis, minicabs, my feet, the Go-Ped, the tube, aeroplanes and railways, in order to access this city, travel about it, and exit it. Not one aspect of my transit has been without its afflictions – and I'm someone who, by and large, has the luxury of planning to take most of my journeys when I want. I only have to think in order to shudder at what it is like for the great majority who're locked into the ebb and flow of the human mill race.

As I read this month's issue of *Stereo on the Go* magazine, I'm driven to the conclusion that ours is a collectivity which, were it an individual, would be immediately diagnosed as an addictive personality. On the contents page the slug lines for one of the pieces blazon: 'Love the M25. When your car is kitted out with in-car movies and games traffic queues are heaven.' This seems to me to be analogous to an alcoholic whiling his time away on a journey to a locked ward in a mental hospital by sinking a few bottles of Hooch.

Of course, such lust for autogeddon is nothing new. I recall 12 years ago, when I had the great misfortune to be a jacket-on-hook, BiSoDol-on-the-dashboard man myself, discussing with a colleague his daily commute. He worked just off the northern extremity of the M25 in Hertford-shire, and lived on the far side of the mighty lake of masonry in Surrey. Every day he would circumnavigate the M25, sometimes clockwise, sometimes anti-clockwise. As the mood took him. It never seemed to occur to this modern Minotaur to pay out a figurative ball of string behind his speeding Sierra, and then follow it back up into the clear light of day.

Apparently Tony Blair was greatly distressed recently when he found himself in the prime-ministerial limo speed-ing down the new buses-and-taxis-only lane which has been created on the M4 between Heathrow and the Chiswick flyover. Whipping past the electorate – he rightly surmised – is a sure-fire way of whipping us up. He resolved to do something about it and issued a proclama-tion via his top poodle, Alastair Campbell, forthwith. Good to know the prime minister wants us all to wade in the same shit, since his current policies are so adept at pumping it out.

Not that anyone in the building professions should be complacent. There's absolutely no point in slapping a building up, if nobody can reach its purlieus. As a member of the public I can surmise that one of the reasons you lot are held in such low esteem, is that subconsciously *we* realise that it's *you* who're responsible for all those clogged up roads, just as much as the infill.

SPEER OF DESTINY

Woody Allen once wrote a sketch called 'The Schmeed Memoirs', which purported to be recollections of Hitler's barber. The opening line of the piece was: 'I did not know Hitler was a Nazi, the truth is for years I thought he worked for the phone company.'

Preposterous as this may sound, the real-life basis for the joke was the publication, in the late 1960s, of the memoirs of Hitler's architect, Albert Speer. *Inside the Third Reich** was a remorseless account of the regime. Speer spent the 20 years of his imprisonment in Spandau setting down on toilet paper, cigarette paper, and just about any other thin surface he could lay his hands on, the details of his close – not to say intense – relationship with Hitler. The glaring peculiarity about these recollections is that nowhere in them does Speer admit to knowledge of the Final Solution, or any of the myriad horrors of the Holocaust. These, he claimed, came winging in on him as he sat in the dock at Nuremberg.

Speer was a good-looking, tall, patrician character, whose impeccable manner embodied what Hitler most admired in the German upper classes. If you like, he was a projection of what Hitler himself might have liked to be. From their initial, chance meeting in 1933, Speer became

*Macmillan, 1999.

one of Hitler's closest confidantes. After the death of Hitler's 'official' architect, Troost, in 1934, Speer had to be on hand at all times of the day and night, should Hitler wish to discuss architectural plans.

Speer had gained his toehold within the regime by doing some conversion work on new Nazi party offices, but he further impressed Hitler with his monumental 'decorative' schemes for the party rallies. The most famous of these was the 'Cathedral of Light' he devised for the 1934 Party congress. This employed every single anti-aircraft search-light Speer could lay his hands on to create an enormous framework of vertically projected beams, below which the massed ranks of the Nazi party banners appeared vast and immemorial. In his memoirs Speer cynically remarked that his lighting aimed to conceal the paunches of the marching Nazis.

It's an irony we can now, if not exactly enjoy, at any rate appreciate, that it was through this insubstantial creation that Speer was given the opportunity to dally with Hitler's more preposterous visions, such as the remodelling of Berlin as 'Germania', the putative capital of the Thousand Year Reich. At the height of their mutually masturbatory architectural dreaming, Speer had an enormous 'model hall', which Hitler would visit for hours at a time, in order to stare at scaled-down projections of an inflated future.

It's for these structures-that-never-were that Speer is chiefly remembered: the huge, overblown, representational buildings which were intended to line the boulevards of the new capital. With their pumped-up proportions and cheesy grandeur, these are examples of neoclassicism afflicted with a pituitary disorder. In fact, hideous to relate, Speer himself did consider his work to be a reaction against the 'perversions' of the Bauhaus, the tendency of modernism to lose itself, as he saw it, in impersonal design.

Speer never, thank heavens, got to make the nightmare of 'Germania' a reality. Instead, he continued to ascend the slippery and viciously barbed pole of the Nazi hierarchy, until he became minister with overall responsibility for economic production. In effect the material boss of Nazi Germany. But despite this, and despite a direct responsibility for the mechanics of the forced labour used to build the V1 and V2 rockets, Speer remained curiously ignorant of the Holocaust.

Throughout the 720 pages of Gita Sereny's fine biography of Speer (*Albert Speer: His Battle With the Truth**), again and again she returns to this seemingly bizarre zone of ignorance. Again and again, Speer, his wife, and other former Nazis Sereny spoke to would make remarks of the form: 'You just don't understand – these are things we didn't speak of.'

Wouldn't it be peculiar if we lived in a world in which it was genocide that was exposed, discussed, publicised and generally dwelt on; while monumental, fascistic architectural schemes were effectively ignored? In such a world Woody Allen might quip: 'I did not know Hitler was an architect ...'

But hang on a minute – perhaps that is this world?

*Vintage, 1996.

THE SENSUOUS PICTS

Mike, a taciturn and hard-knapping garden sculptor, has just about finished building a replica of a Pictish brough or fortified dwelling house, in our back garden. It stands some eight feet high and is approximately four-and-a-half feet in diameter. In outline it displays the profile of a power station cooling tower, with the walls bellying out slightly, before dipping in towards the top. This curve – a flattened 'S' – is marvellously sensuous in the original, and Mike has achieved the fantastic feat of reproducing it in our replica.

Why a brough?, is of course the question most frequently asked nowadays by visitors *chez* Self. Most of the answer is aesthetic; the very shape of the thing is a fluid antidote to the cuboid structures which dominate the contemporary built environment (with one notable exception we'll come to later). By employing slate, rather than the sandstone used for the originals, Mike has been able to recreate the textural quality of the original brough on a far smaller scale. This is, again, an aspect of the brough infrequently embodied in our urban scape: the harmonisation of naturally defined materials with a human living environment. It is this essential harmony – I would hazard – that makes the brough so pleasing to the eye.

The broughs were built by the Picts between the first and fourth centuries AD. Remains of about 300 have been found scattered around the northern coast of Scotland and the northern isles. But the only fully intact brough is on the Isle of Mousa, off the coast of Shetland. The Brough of Mousa stands some 60 feet high. You enter through a small door and find yourself in a courtyard open to the sky. There is an inner wall to the brough, and it was in this interstitial space that the chambers the Picts lived in are found. Opposite the door is the entrance to a stairwell, where conventional, switch-backing flights of stairs mount to the upper parapet at the top. This entire structure is dry stone.

Some archeologists theorise that these were fortified dwelling houses, and that a clan would retreat into a brough at time of siege, the cattle occupying the courtyard. Other archeologists suggest that the broughs were roofed with wooden platforms, which catapults like Roman *ballistae* sat on. They cite, in support of this contention, the fact that many broughs are in pairs, placed either side of sea channels or inlets. In fact, no evidence has been found at any brough site of any kind of armed assault upon them. Could it be that these were ultimately successful deterrents?

I doubt it. My hunch is that the Picts simply liked living in broughs because they're bloody marvellous buildings. I'd like to live in a brough. I'd like to see some full-size brough reconstructions, following Mike's trail-blazing. The only contemporary circular building that's currently grabbing popular attention represents absolutely no harmony between the human and the natural, and has all the aesthetic merits of a boil.

IMMEMORIAL TEENAGERS

I wrote a while back about the Pictish brough, or fortified dwelling house, which I have had built in my back garden in London. I'm glad to say that this piece garnered quite a response from readers. One man phoned to tell me that he was planning to build a full-size reconstruction of a brough in Northumberland, and an architect in Shetland was in touch about his broch (he champions this spelling), which conceals an oil tank on the island of Vaila.

The brough has an intrinsically pleasing shape; and although they were probably designed for defensive purposes, all the ones I've been inside have a distinctly good feeling about them. None more so than the remains of Midhowe brough on the Orkney island of Rousay – where I'm currently staying. Inside this brough you can find such evidence of cheerful domesticity as a cistern and an ancient quern, both, of course, resolutely stone.

Next to the brough on this isolated, rugged island, is a far more imposing and charged megalith. This is the chambered, or stalled, tomb of Midhowe, a huge pod shape of layered stones, with a central chamber some hundred feet long; which must – when the tomb was intact – have risen to ten feet in height; the massive, corbelled walls meeting in a high arch. The tomb was built around 2500 BC – and by the time the Pictish brough builders happened along, nearly 3000 years later, it must have been little more than a grassed-over mound.

It's an astonishing building; all the more astonishing when you discover that it took many many generations to construct; that it was in use for at least 1000 years; and that it was found, sealed up, with the bones of only 19 individuals inside. Even though I've visited the tomb many times, I seldom actually venture inside the protective building which has been erected over it – the atmosphere is that unsettling.

There are all sorts of explanations as to why the megalithic tombs were made as they were, but the fact most salient is surely the time and labour involved in building them, and this at a time when it's estimated that the average life expectancy of the populace was only in the late teens. One would have to conclude that the design of the completed tomb was in some fashion transmitted down through the successive generations – how could this be so?

Some theorists have proposed the existence of a neolithic 'yard' or universal measure around which the megalithic tombs were constructed, but I think it far more likely that these were people who were less melded into individual consciousnesses than us moderns. Indeed, I'd go so far as to suggest that the tombs were built more in the way that hives are evolved by social insects, than the way country houses are planned by commissioned architects.

Mind you, some archeologist of the distant future might well conclude the same about us, when she comes to excavate such apparently purposeless and monumental structures as the British motorway system.

THE ALL-SEEING EYE

Strictly speaking, the five-spoked British prisons, such as
HMP Wandsworth in London, and HMP Strangeways in
Manchester, are not built exactly according to the panopticon principles of Jeremy Bentham. As I understand it the
great Utilitarian's idea was for an entirely circular prison,
in which all the cells were accessed through a central well
from where the warders could observe all of the prisoners
all of the time.

Bentham thought the panopticon design would reinforce the notion of a benevolent and omniscient god in the
morally benighted minds of the incarcerated; but the five-
spoked meta-panopticons were conceived rather in the
spirit of a riot-controlling deity. The great advantage of
having each wing leading off from a central hub, is that
trouble in any one of them can be seen from the centre. If
it develops, the wing can be sealed, then reinforcements
can be brought up entirely from within the prison building itself.

I know that prison is not intended to be a picnic – not
even the open ones. But for rank despair, as expressed by a
building, you couldn't do much better than the panopti-
cons. I remember having the good fortune to end up at the
heels of Judge Stephen Tumin, then chief inspector of prisons, as he made an unscheduled tour of Wandsworth.
Being chief inspector of anything has to be about the best

job in the world. Tumin certainly took full advantage of it: steaming up to prisoners and asking to eat their lunch; forcing prison officers to show him their duty rosters; and all the while making pointed and acerbic remarks. Terrific.

At that time the notorious 'slopping out' had just been finished, and the remaining lineaments of the Victorian gaol were being speedily clothed in painted steel, MDF and acres of chipboard. They had also, in the wake of the Strangeways riots, taken it upon themselves to seal off some of the spokes, on the grounds that it was the only way to stop trouble spilling over into the rest of the prison. I took this comprehensive piece of conversion at face value, as a derogation of the Benthamite principle: henceforth it would be useless to continually observe all the prisoners, on the grounds that the staff probably didn't want to know what they were up to anyway.

Of course, prisons are no longer built according to these antiquated, moralistic notions. If you go down to the Isle of Sheppey you can see three absolutely terrific modern prisons, all within one pan across the blank horizon. These prisons, with their anti-climb walls, and steel roofs, look like industrial units designed for the assembly line production of recidivists.

And if you're in Northern Ireland you can pop up and have a gander at the outside of the Maze. Here architecture and sectarian politics have coincided, so that I doubt that anyone in their right mind will consider designing an 'H'-shaped place of confinement ever again.

I once had the incredible misfortune to be imprisoned for a night in a two-berth sleeping compartment on the Inverness Express from Euston. I say misfortune, because my companion was an alcoholic prison guard who had suffered a mental breakdown after being held hostage for 12 days during the Strangeways riots. After emptying with three gulps the whiskey bottle I had foolishly offered him, he fixed me with a manic eye and said: 'Have you any idea what it's like to be trapped in a confined space with some-one who's violently mad?'

Well, I do now. And I think I know what's happened to the ousted concept of the panopticon. A couple of days ago I found myself sitting in a central well which provided me with a comprehensive view of five spoke-like wings. I watched the inmates hurrying this way and that, buying sweets and hamburgers, going to the toilet. They didn't seem unduly distressed – or no more so than you would expect, given that they were in a service centre on the M4.

BACK TO THE FUTURE

Drugs and architecture – not things that you would have considered bed mates, or even mind mates. Yet drugs and architecture do have a profound connection, and in one particular cultural development it could be argued that drugs were responsible for transmuting the aesthetics of architecture. I refer to the Romantics and their notion of the sublime.

Thomas De Quincey in his *Confessions of an English Opium Eater* tells us that initially: 'The splendours of my (opium) dreams were indeed chiefly architectural; and I beheld such pomp of cities and palaces as was never yet beheld by the waking eye, unless in the clouds.' Latterly, however, the architectural came to be regarded by De Quincey through the darkening lens of his drug addiction, and to represent the awful aspect of the sublime, rather than the ineffable or the expansive. The entire passage De Quincey wrote, influenced by the tormented engravings of Piranesi, is too long to quote in this context. However, the essence of it is that De Quincey found himself, in these visions, in 'vast Gothic halls: on the floor of which stood all sorts of engines and machinery; wheels, cables, pulleys, levers, catapults, etc. etc. Expressive of enormous power put forth and resistance overcome.'

De Quincey witnessed an Escher-style confusion of perspective: 'Creeping along the sides of the walls you perceived a staircase; and upon it, groping his way upwards, was Piranesi himself: follow the steps a little further, and you perceive it come to a sudden abrupt termination, without any balustrade ... Whatever is to become of poor Piranesi ... But raise your eyes, and behold a second flight of stairs still higher: on which again Piranesi is perceived, but this time standing on the very brink of the abyss.'

Of course, De Quincey was not alone in seeing vast structures and illimitable spaces (or perhaps imagining he saw them, opium is after all a narcotic rather than an hallucinogen), his one-time friend, the poet Coleridge, famously wrote *Kubla Khan*, inspired by opium and freighted the poem with notions of the architectural sublime. I certainly don't believe that either man's visions were the product of opium alone; to quote De Quincey again: 'If a man who keeps oxen should take opium, he will dream of oxen.'

No, rather the interesting question is, what was it about architecture – of a particular kind – that so obsessed the English romantics? What was it that it represented? I believe the answer is both novel and disturbing.

It's notable that the architectural visions of De Quincey were focused exclusively on large-scale architecture. Indeed, for De Quincey the evocation of a small-scale – if not *gemütlich* – interior was the very essence of calm and security. But if the visions of endless confused buildings terrorised him, it was in his contemplation of the potential tenants of these buildings that De Quincey really began to lose it.

De Quincey had always had an ambivalent attitude towards crowds. Although in the early sections of the *Confessions*, his chief 'opium pleasure' was to sample the delights of the *boulevardier,* by wandering the streets of central London; as the addiction took hold, the very notion of the mass of people became anathema to him. His phobia zeroed in on the oriental, a culture then new to the west, but for which De Quincey conceived a peculiar, pre-emptive hatred: 'It contributes much to these feelings, that Southern Asia is, and has been for thousands of years, the part of the earth most swarming with life; the great *officina gentium.* Man is a weed in these regions.'

Great halls full of redundant machinery suggesting 'enormous power put forth and resistance overcome'; a sense of perspective cheated by the vertiginous; and a notion of humanity being 'a weed', presumably entwined in the architecture, both choking and choked by it. To my mind these narcotic reveries of 170 years ago imply one thing and one thing alone: the overpopulated modern city as it has become in the twentieth century.

Yes, it may seem preposterous, but I think De Quincey's visions were of the future; a future he could perceive already in the pullulation of London as it expanded with cancerous alacrity throughout the nineteenth century. Pre-posterous, if you don't know that much about De Quincey, but remember this is the man who delineated the concept of the unconscious mind and its relation to repression, some 40 years before Freud was born!

'There's nothing complex about your inferiority …'

A COTE DU CHEZ SELF

My computer man, Toby, came round the other day, and while some of his digitised vaccines were operating on the disordered memory of my virtual desktop, he fell to examining a copy of a book which was kicking around the actual one. 'This looks great, Will,' he said 'look at these photos.' The book in question was Alex de Rijke's *On The Road*, an overview of a touring exhibition he mounted, together with the Architecture Foundation, on 'the art of engineering in the car age'.

Rijke's small book is indeed 'great'. It's an exemplary coupling of lucid, precise, descriptive prose; interesting but not overworked technical details; and splendidly laconic photography of the engineering art by Rijke himself.

The reason why it had been lying around on the desk for months, was that although the author had himself given me a copy at last year's *Building Design* Awards, and I'd averred that I would most certainly read it, I'd completely forgotten about it.

Not much new about that. It could well be the many, many years I've spent well over the herbaceous borders of the psyche, or simply that the meagre storehouses of my mind have long since been filled, but nowadays I can remember hardly anything. The Elizabethans devised involved architectural mnemonics they called 'memory theatres', in which they could stash their recollections. It's

a beautiful concept; a transliteration of the farouche ideal-
ism of the Platonic cave, into a proto-Enlightenment
palace of entertainment. However, the nearest I could get
to such a structure would be a multiplex of amnesia.

In *Hannibal*, his long-awaited sequel to *The Silence of
the Lambs*, Thomas Harris goes in some detail into the
fantastic 'memory palace' his protagonist, the polymath
psychopath Hannibal Lecter, has built for himself during
his decades of solitary confinement: 'The palace is built
according to the rules discovered by Simonides of Ceos
and elaborated by Cicero 400 years later; it is airy, high-
ceilinged, furnished with objects and tableaux that are
vivid, striking, sometimes shocking and absurd, and often
beautiful. The displays are well spaced and well lighted
like those of a great museum. But the walls are not the neu-
tral colours of museum walls. Like Giotto, Dr Lecter has
frescoed the walls of his mind.'

Far from frescoing its walls, for most of the time I feel as
if I've allowed a bull coated with Artex to run amok in my
memory tea shop, so unlike Lecter's edifice of lucidity do
its cramped, cluttered confines feel. Harris tells us that
Lecter's palace 'is vast ... Translated to the tangible world
it would rival the Tokapi Palace in Istanbul for size and
complexity.' Hmm, if we didn't know already that Lecter
was a raving, ravening raptor, this grandiose reification of
his mind would give it away, reminding us as it must of
another monster with a fine memory for architectural
detail.

'... witnesses would confirm how knowledgeable Hitler
was. According to Speer, he could draw the Ring Boulevard (in Vienna) and the adjoining districts with the large
buildings true to scale and from memory ... Indeed, as

eyewitnesses noticed with astonishment in 1940 in Paris, he had precise knowledge of the great buildings in Paris, in particular of the Opera' (Brigitte Hamann, *Hitler's Vienna*). Hitler's feverish, late-adolescent peregrinations around the kitsch capital of the Hapsburgs furnished him with a bizarre ideological mnemonic which he referred to for the rest of his life. He described the Ring as 'the most beautiful line of streets that has ever been built on old entrenchments, with buildings that, to be sure, were designed in eclectic styles, but by idiosyncratic and good architects, and thus without any epigenous decadence.'

Now, while I wouldn't want to assert that everyone with this three-dimensional memory of the built environment is a Hitler, or a Lecter in the making, I do think those of us who are incapable of accurately depicting a building which we're standing directly in front of, are far closer to the human mean. Which brings us, rather neatly, back to *On the Road* in which de Rijke discusses the Stockwell Bus Garage, a triumphant piece of modernism, built in 1950 and designed by Adie Buttons & Partners with Thomas Bilbow. I live around the corner from said garage, I walk around it every day. I (allegedly) write a column on architecture, and yet, if you asked me to the draw the thing from memory all I'd come up with is a scrawl which looked like a squeezy bottle coupling with a dolphin.

Makes yer fink, dunnit?

SCREEN MEMORIES

Wow! This is as boring as people telling you their dreams, but I've just encountered an astonishing effect on my computer … Asleep yet? You poor techie nerd. But anyway, when I switch from the ludicrously facile – but for all that endlessly useful – Encarta Encyclopaedia CD-ROM to my word-processing programme, for a few brief instants, the photograph of the famous Court of the Lions in the Alhambra (the reason why I am consulting this particular entry will become abundantly clear below, should you choose to hang on to consciousness for that long) becomes colour variegated in the most astonishing fashion: a pointillist stippling and a Pollock-splattering of the spectra invades each detail of Mohammed the Fifth's eternal patio, so as to create a perfect, instantaneous Monet. I kid you not – try it on your system. You can make your own Monet out of almost any image there is on Encarta.

But anyway, as my favourite beat combo Massive Attack would warble: 'Inertia comes creeping up slowly', and my little trip-hop through the mountainous grooves of the CD-ROM is all by way of anticipating what I hope will be a year of very real travelling. Last year I managed to hit cities in Europe and North America in the course of my travels, but the architectural highlights were incidental rather than planned, a gasp at the buttress of that venerable cathedral, a gawp at the mirrored flank of this cloud-topping modern behemoth. My attempts to view the built environment are like someone reading a copy of Pevsner on acid. Not for me the structured trip to see the structure. Not never.

This year however, plans have already been laid between my architect friend Christopher and myself, for the two of us and our consorts to visit Istanbul in search of the city's ancient, architectural aesthetics. Indeed, plans are now so well advanced that he telephoned me the other day to say that he'd managed to get the hotel rooms we particularly wanted – overlooking the Tulip Mosque. Doesn't that sound fantastic? 'The rooms overlooking the Tulip Mosque'; such a ring. And it's right there as well that my whole delusion about me, travel and architecture, starts to waver and dissolve into a Monet-like vision of Giverny (which, as you recall, is a plot the size of an allotment, now bounded by an eight-lane *péage*).

It's Christopher whose suggestion this was; Christopher who's proposed the dates; Christopher who even knows of the existence of the Tulip Mosque – and the possibility of an hotel room overlooking it. I couldn't plan a trip to Coventry if I tried. I am as contrary to the idea of visiting a place/building/natural scene in any rational fashion as it is possible for a person to be. I have no clear idea why this should be, but take the following brief checklist as staggering evidence of my wilful determination to avoid the highpoints.

India, 1984. A surprisingly clean-cut Self detrains at Agra, fully intent on sampling the delights of the Taj Mahal. However, *en route* to the world's toppermost mausoleum I am distracted by a copy of Henry Miller's *Tropic of Cancer*, which is being mysteriously offered for sale by an amputee in the gutter. Four hours later I entrain once more for New Delhi, the Taj Mahal unvisited.

Grenada, Spain, 1985. I detrain intent on basking among the cool fountains of the Alhambra. There is a copy of the *Seven Pillars of Wisdom* in my haversack and nothing is going to come between me and one of the great aesthetic experiences of my life. Nothing, that is, save for a greasy paella and a bottle of gut-Rioja. After three toilet-bound hours I retrain, paradise unvisited.

Athens, 1992. A funny thing happens on the way to the Acropolis. I pause on the steep path up to the very incarnation of classicism, and feeling the need to assuage a hangover of Illiadic proportions pop into a taverna, the rest as they say is ... history.

This year it will be different. Please.

AUTHOR'S NOTE: It wasn't.

NORTH STAND, DELPHI

As I write, a vast segment of the nation is gearing itself up for either triumph or defeat; unalloyed pleasure or puling discontent. The weirdest thing about the World Cup, as far as I'm concerned, is that for the best part of each interim four-year period I'm as indifferent to the great game as I am to the mating practises of the halibut. Actually, I'll correct that: I'm marginally more interested in halibut sex. Indeed, if you were to ask me to tell one end of a football from another, I think I'd have the greatest difficulty in even making an inspired guess.

But I'm no more immune to the pull of mass events than anybody else, and this World Cup has proved no exception. For a few brief weeks I have found myself admitted to this country-wide sodality, wherein it's quite acceptable to turn to people, in public, who you don't know at all, and start discussing the relative merits of various formations and whether or not the former Yugoslavia might have done better if they'd employed a more vigorous sweeper system.

Why should this be? Obviously I'm not going to trouble you with a great dollop of socio-psychology and cultural anthropology – that's not the role of this column, but some of the things about these mondial events are rooted firmly in the architectural.

The idea that many many thousands of English football

fans are prepared to travel to French towns where they will get no closer to a live view of the action than an enormous, direct-relay screen set up outside the ground, puts the whole event in its correct context: that of a religious ceremony. Eat it, drink it, dream it, breathe it – so the advertisements exhort us. But the one imprecation they dare not – cannot – make, is to abjure us to worship football and to pray to the great globular god.

Yet would this really be as blasphemous as it seems on first examination? The predicament of the unticketed fans hanging around the precincts of the stadium puts me in mind, most strongly, of the similar predicament of ancient Greeks denied entry to the original olympiads held at Delphi all those seasons ago. The Greeks had the right idea – and we've inherited it. The excellence of the body and the excellence of the spirit are in many ways coextensive, and the competitions the Greeks devised to demonstrate the former took place within structures which embodied the latter.

I vividly remember my trip to Delphi. The location is superb, the jumble of ancient buildings cupped in a fold of Mount Parnassus and looking out upon wave after wave of blue-green hill tops. Deep within the ruins of the temple of Apollo lies the adyton, or vault where the Pythia, the girl oracle, would reside while she formulated her prophecies. Of course, there was a priesthood on hand to interpret the strange gabblings of the Pythia, and as people came from all over the ancient world to consult the oracle, it acted as a news service, as well as a form of prognostication.

The inscriptions over the temple door – 'Know thyself', 'Do not exceed', and 'The mean is best' – have a not unsporting aspect to them. In among the temples dedicated to the gods and goddesses of the pantheon, there was a small but perfectly formed stadium. A key part of the Delphic ceremonies were these races, discus throws and javelin launches. I shouldn't imagine that the Greeks made much distinction between the chthonic activities of the oracle and the callisthenic activities of the athletes.

Perhaps a good solution to the problems of tribalism, defunct nationalism, and all-round testosterone-fuelled looniness that seem to afflict contemporary mass sporting events would be for Delphi to permanently host the World Cup; and make the ancient ceremonials a central aspect of the tournament.

This would create ticket-allocation problems but as far as I can see, the reason why this is currently so contentious is that modern stadia continually taunt us with their size. 'What!', we exclaim internally when we see the venue for the next match. 'You mean to say it's impossible to fit more than a couple of thousand of us into that great bowl of concrete?' Yes, as ever, it's modernism that's to blame. Return sport to its original architectural scale and none of this trouble could even get underway.

'I was virtually a child when I built this place ...'

NOISY MACHINERY – SILENT MONITOR

As a child I was preoccupied with the notion of idealised communities – utopias if you will. During prepuberty my interest took the form of constructing elaborate settlements out of Lego, building blocks and cardboard boxes. The dwellings were connected with one another by vertiginous string cable-car lines, along which plastic and rubber figurines – the inhabitants – were unsteadily winched.

Perhaps the most obvious inspiration for these activities was the beneficence of King Babar. As you will recall, Babar built Celesteville as a fully incorporated and planned development, in which all the – admittedly crude – buildings were in harmony with one another.

As I grew older, and became increasingly bookish, my fantasies took flight into the past. I began to read about the idealised communities of the nineteenth century, the phalansteries of Fourrier, and the post-industrial paradises of Saint-Simon. But the utopia that most grabbed my attention – because it had, unlike the above, actually existed – was the mill-based community of New Lanark in Scotland.

New Lanark was originally built by a Glasgow banker, cotton factor and philanthropist, David Dale. Dale spotted the enormous hydraulic-power potential represented by the Falls of Clyde which lie below Lanark. In partnership with Richard Arkwright, the inventor and pioneer of industrial cotton spinning, Dale commenced the building of the first mill at New Lanark in 1785. Although weirs had to be constructed upstream, and a 1000-foot tunnel cut through solid rock to channel the water, spinning began the following year. By 1793 four mills had been built and 1100 people were employed. Despite many vicissitudes, cotton continued to be spun there until 1968.

Because of the inaccessible nature of the site, Dale needed to have his workforce *in situ*. This led to the construction of the tremendous terraces of tenement apartments which are still standing to this day. The absence of flat ground, and the limitations of the plots Dale had bought, meant that the entire settlement was lain out in sinuous lines which follow the contours of the steep valley sides. At Dale's insistence the buildings were roofed with slate rather than thatch, because of its greater durability. Built using heavy amounts of rendering, with 12-paned windows, and ranging between three and six storeys in height, the buildings of New Lanark have a pleasing, cool uniformity; the Georgian and the vernacular.

Is it too fanciful to suggest that it was Dale's buildings which provided the necessary crucibles within which Robert Owen's notions of 'village(s) of unity and mutual cooperation' could take root? Owen pitched up in New Lanark in 1798, a young man familiar with industrial processes, and on the look out for a suitable place for social experimentation. He assumed management of the mill the following year and married Dale's daughter Caroline.

Owen began to construct a vision of philanthropy working alongside commercial advantage. 'All the houses in the village,' he wrote, 'form parts of the establishment, all united and working together as one machine, proceeding day by day with the regularity of clockwork.'

Owen systematised the management procedures; detailed records were kept of productivity and costs. On a more sinister note, Owen introduced his famous 'silent monitor', a four-sided block of wood that dangled above each worker. Each side was a different colour, indicating a different level of work performance. If the black side of the monitor was displayed your work was poor, and Owen would give you a penetrating glare. It sounds oppressive, but of course in any other industrial combine of the time you might well have received a beating. Owen also introduced a sick fund, a savings bank and a store, as well as universal education. Indeed, the latter formed the basis of the primary-school system as we know it today.

Eventually Owen ran out of luck. His attempt to construct an American community along Owenite lines, New Harmony, failed to find sufficient backing. Owen himself might have adduced political and economic reasons for the failure of New Harmony, but I would be inclined to point to architectural ones. There's a model of the proposed New Harmony community at New Lanark, and it shows a Victorian incarnation of the Renaissance 'radiant city'. Unlike the graceful, sinuous terraces of New Lanark, New Harmony appears soulless and institutional.

New Lanark now has a second lifetime as a World Heritage Site, and you can stay in a marvellous hotel which has been opened in the reconstructed No. 1 mill building. The village is still a working community – albeit largely the work of tourism. I can't think of any other 200-year-old utopias that are still functioning in any way shape or form – though I understand Celesteville is advertising for new settlers. But only those with big trunks need apply.

PHOBIAGROUND

When I was a child, growing up in The Hampstead Garden Suburb in north London, I was allowed to run more or less free from the age of five. It was considered slightly dangerous to cross the North Circular Road – it had only two lanes then – and visit the local playground, but it was not by any means forbidden. The playground was absolutely of its time: asphalted, with entirely iron apparatus of swings, roundabout, witch's hat roundabout, see-saw, and climbing frame. At the base of each of these potential death traps was a pediment of paving stones; as if this represented a better cushioning surface than asphalt. On one occasion, standing on top of the climbing frame, I pitched forward head first, and fell eight feet, colliding with numerous iron bars on my way down.

The playground was completely unsupervised. It was as if, in the mid-1960s, the sexual abuse of minors simply didn't happen. By the same token, at age seven I was allowed to take the underground 12 stops to school, alone; and by the time I was 11 I had, more or less, the run of the entire city. This was not – I hasten to add – because my parents were especially neglectful; it was simply the character of the times.

Now, when I take my children (aged seven and five) to the playground, I note the security camera on its priapic pole (somewhat mimicking what it's there to prevent); I note the wood chips or resilient rubber that surrounds the playground apparatus; and I adhere to the injunction not to smoke. At our local adventure playground one of the large wooden slides is sponsored by Abacus Self Storage; and there is an 'organic garden'. The last time we were there the children were offered the opportunity to 'make an alien'.

In the late 1970s and early 1980s I had the dubious job title 'senior play leader' and ran a play scheme for the GLC. Together with James Lampard – a co-founder of the Portsmouth Symphonia, along with Brian Eno – I built enormous inflatable structures, and then carted them around the London parks. These inflatables were the opposite of bouncy castles: their object seemed to be to expel, rather than contain children who were propelled into the air. Our favourite was an H-shaped assembly of tubes, some ten feet high. When too many children were bouncing on the cross section of the 'H', the kids on the uprights would be thrown high into the air. We averaged something like 200 children per session on the inflatables; and often twice that number. We had five supervisory staff, tops. In four years of running the scheme I only remember there being one serious injury – a broken arm.

Nowadays middle-class children are effectively barred from public spaces. They are shepherded to and from school in Volvos with side impact protection systems; and in playgrounds their natural grace is circumscribed by intensive supervision by parents, cameras, and youth workers. It would be an impossible statistic to contrive, but I'd wager that there are no fewer accidents in these cushioned environments than there were in the old concrete jungles.

It appears to me that we are fashioning our children's sense of the built environment through projection of our own fears: of sex abusers, of car accidents, and of physical injury. Playgrounds – even the more 'adventurous' kind – are really phobiagrounds, in which children learn to fear the world they live in, and accept a future in which they will live in 'gated' communities, protected from the rest of society by armed security guards.